SYNECTICS

The Development of Creative Capacity

SYNECTICS

The Development of Creative Capacity

BY WILLIAM J. J. GORDON

Harper & Brothers · Publishers · New York

SYNECTICS

First Edition

K-L

TO M. S. G.

CONTENTS

ACKNOWLEDGMENTS

In the course of almost two decades of research I have received encouragement and immeasurable assistance from a wide variety of people.

Prof. Donald Gifford (Williams College): Mr. Gifford first began discussing the creative process with me in Africa in 1943. His enthusiasm for this project has continued, and in 1959 he not only worked through certain aspects of this book with me but actually wrote out his views, many of which have been integrated into the text. Mr. Gifford's contribution is particularly significant in the chapter devoted to the use of metaphor.

Mr. Carlton Marden (Invention-Research Group): In the course of working with Mr. Marden for over twelve years I learned much about how, in the process of reducing a concept to practice, the object that is being constructed begins to have a life of its own; and that successful invention depends on permitting the object to act with sufficient autonomy to guide the inventor.

Mr. Robert Jalkovsky (Arthur D. Little, Inc.): Mr. Jalkovsky's contribution results from his capacity to generalize about thought processes in specific problem-solving situations. In the early days of Synectics research his insights continually forced me to plumb more deeply into the actual psychological states underlying constructive imagination.

Mr. Richard Foster (Harvard University): Mr. Foster has been a willing and encouraging companion in a sequence of research adventures. His eagerness and optimism carried us through a multitude of setbacks and disappointments.

Prof. Jerome Bruner (Harvard University): Mr. Bruner, more than anyone else, triggered the compilation of this book. He persuaded me that it should be written and when I suggested that he be the one to write it, he refused. Since his persuasion had committed me, there was nothing for it but to get to work on it myself.

Dr. Robert Morrison (Rockefeller Foundation): During one of many meetings at the Rockefeller Foundation, Mr. Morrison told me that unless Synectics theory could be simplified it would be worthless. His tough-minded criticism was never forgotten and the chapter on psychological mechanisms is the resulting attempt at clarity and simplicity.

Dr. Robert Burden (Harvard University): Over a period of years Mr. Burden has cheered this project on. At a time when there was no measurable reason for confidence he was reassuring. After the theory had been tested and appeared valid he became a constructive critic and adviser. It is difficult for me to be explicit about Mr. Burden's help because his constant championship is so subtle that often I have been made aware of it only accidentally.

Dr. Donald Schone (Arthur D. Little, Inc.): Shortly after Mr. Schone joined the group in 1958 he became interested in the question of how some men repeatedly choose a line of thought which leads to a successful solution. His inquiry into this aspect of creative process motivated our joint development of the importance of Hedonic Response.

Mr. George Prince (Invention-Research Group): Mr. Prince's insistence on the necessity of intelligibility for the purpose of Synectics training programs was the direct cause of the most important single advance in theory. Before Mr. Prince joined the research effort, we were dragged down with abstractions and ill-defined impressions. His evocative and demanding influence led to a degree of concreteness and distinctness which never would have come to pass without his presence.

Mr. C. Richard Sperry (Invention-Research Group): Mr. Sperry's attitude toward research is a continuing lesson in decision making. Time after time he has jerked projects out of inactive speculation into constructive building and testing.

The operating Synectics groups in Kimberly-Clark, Singer Sewing Machine Co., Johns-Manville, and RCA-Whirlpool serve as a continuing source of feedback knowledge. Synectics theory has benefitted immeasurably from all these relationships since they constitute the laboratories where new insights are tested in a functional environment. Particular appreciation goes to William Wilson of Kimberly-Clark, who was the leader of the first test group. The fact that he survived the initial Synectics experiment speaks more for his stubborn courage than for the effectiveness of Synectics theory when it was in its infancy.

Permission to use the word "Synectics" has been granted by Synectics, Inc., of Cambridge, Massachusetts.

SYNECTICS
The Development of Creative Capacity

INTRODUCTION

The word *Synectics*, from the Greek, means the joining together of different and apparently irrelevant elements. Synectics theory applies to the integration of diverse individuals into a problem-stating problem-solving group. It is an operational theory for the conscious use of the preconscious psychological mechanisms present in man's creative activity. The purpose of developing such a theory is to increase the probability of success in problem-stating, problem-solving situations. This increase depends on awareness of the mechanisms which must be worked through to arrive at solutions of fundamental novelty. (Novelty is fundamental to the degree that it is general. A special cam may be a new way to make a particular apparatus function better, but this cam is not applicable to any other piece of apparatus. A transistor, on the other hand, is applicable to a wide range of uses.)

The study of creative process is encumbered by the fact that, being a process, it is in motion. Traditionally, creative process has been considered after the fact—halted for observation. But when the process is stopped, what is there to observe? The Synectics study has attempted to research creative process in vivo, while it is going on. To understand the digestion process of a cow it is possible to put a picture window in the cow's stomach(s). However, a window opening onto the brain of a man who is acting creatively would be useless because not enough is understood about the brain to know what we would be seeing. Therefore, the only way to learn about creative process is to try to gain insight into the underlying, non-rational, free-associative concepts which flow under the articulated surface phenomena. To do this, Synectics research has required problems to be solved and people to be observed.

The Cambridge Synectics group, which was the first and is a continuing source of the data and hypotheses examined in this book, enjoys a symbiotic relationship with industry. In spite of substantial assistance of many kinds from personnel at the Department of Defense, the Institute of Contemporary Art, the Rockefeller Foundation, Harvard University, and Massachusetts Institute of Technology, American industry has become the most prominent laboratory element in Synectics research. The Cambridge Synectics group needs problems to solve and groups with which to work in order to continue its research. Industry needs problems solved and must have creative groups within it to continue producing basic novelty. In the course of this work the Cambridge Synectics group has developed increasing experimental insight into the conception and reduction to practice of radically novel ideas—from observing its own process as well as the process of groups in training.

The present Cambridge Synectics group consists of six men of varied background (physics, mechanics, biology, geology, marketing, and chemistry). Part of their time is spent in sessions attacking invention problems. Tape recordings of successful sessions (where a concept promising enough to test is developed) are analyzed to learn how the concept originated. Another part of their time is devoted to implementation—building working models, conducting experiments, and investigating market potentials. There are frequent discussions of progress which serve two purposes. First, they keep the group in touch with how a project is going. Second, by hearing about how individuals overcome specific problems, more is learned about the invention process. The other activity of the group is teaching. Certain members select candidates and train selectees from client companies in the use of the Synectics method.[1]

The group functions under two leaders. One handles administrative matters; the other guides the sessions themselves. However, there is a high degree of democracy. For example, any member can call together other members of the group for a session, and administrative decisions of any moment are decided by the whole group.

This book is an interim report on research which will continue for years to come. The objective of the research to date has been to develop an operational concept of human creativity and to test this

[1] Wilson, William: "Operational Creativity," Marketing & Transportation Paper No. 2 (Michigan State University, East Lansing, Michigan, 1958).

concept. The conclusions stated and implied in this book form the basis on which other successful Synectics groups have been founded; when a scientific experiment repeatedly yields similar results, such confirmation is held to be a demonstration of the validity of the underlying hypothesis. However, not all the conclusions (although based on experimental evidence) are to be taken as fixed and final, but as hypotheses in transition, suitable for further research and study. Synectics research hinges on the following assumptions:

(i)   that the creative process in human beings can be concretely described and, further, that sound description should be usable in teaching methodology to increase the creative output of both individuals and groups. This assumption places Synectics theory in direct conflict with the theory that any attempt to analyze and train imagination and those aspects of the human psyche associated directly with the creative process threatens the process with destruction. In other words, true analysis of the creative process is considered impossible since if the individual attempts to examine himself in process, the process ceases immediately, and his examination is bankrupt. This theory implies that illumination is destructive. At present this prejudice seems groundless. Synectics' attempts to illuminate the creative process have resulted in several working hypotheses which are useful in practice and have increased markedly the creative output of both individuals and groups;

(ii)   that the cultural phenomena of invention in the arts and in science are analogous and are characterized by the same fundamental psychic processes;

(iii) that individual process in the creative enterprise enjoys a direct analogy in group process.

The purpose of the book is to describe the evolution of Synectics' theory of creative process, the hypotheses that underly the theory, and the actual implementation of the theory in specific cases.

Research: The aim of Synectics research, since 1944, has been to uncover the psychological mechanisms basic to creative activity. The recurrent problem has been how to discover these mechanisms when they were buried within the subjective responses of individuals. The main body of this research consisted of oscillating between gaining concrete insight about the psychological mechanisms and testing the validity of these mechanisms in problem-stating, problem-solving situations. The latest part of Synectics research has been directed toward exploring the use of problem-solving groups trained in the Synectics mechanisms. Test groups are presently operating in a number of American companies with considerable—and increasing—success. This success results from the Synectics mechanisms becoming defined more and more functionally as the research develops along increasingly concrete lines. Growing interest has been shown in the implications of Synectics at all levels of education. Up to now the methodology had to be tested in a practical climate where experiments could be judged on the basis of pragmatic criteria. However, Synectics research is about to be applied experimentally to educational processes as known today in our schools and colleges.

Hypotheses: Synectics theory holds that:

(i)   creative efficiency in people can be markedly increased if they understand the psychological process by which they operate;

(ii)   in creative process the emotional component is more important than the intellectual, the irrational more important than the rational;

(iii)   it is these emotional, irrational elements which can and must be understood in order to increase the probability of success in a problem-solving situation.

Practice: Establishing Synectics problem-stating and problem-solving groups goes through three phases: selection of personnel, training in Synectics, and integration back into the client environment. During the training process from time to time judgments are made of the group's progress by evaluating its solutions to previously unsolved client problems. Although Synectics theory is being applied broadly, a group in training limits its effort to technical problems. Technical solutions can be evaluated more positively than solutions to problems in areas like policy or finance.

Examples: Concrete examples of tape recorded sessions have been chosen to illustrate elements of Synectics in practice. For the benefit of the general reader I have attempted to select examples which do not include highly complex and technical scientific material.

The traditional nineteenth century romantic view of the nature of creativity places heavy emphasis on the fine arts and poetry as the "only" creative enterprise, and asserts the primacy of individual genius in such a way that all human creative experience is hustled into the dark limbo of personal mystery. The common-sense twentieth century view of the creative process has become complicated by insistence on some method of measurement. How can we test for the mysterious quality of "creativity"? How can we single out the creative individual in the democratic mass? How can we train individuals to become creative in the complex societies which we call education or industry? In other words, the twentieth century view of creativity is bifurcated into, on the one hand, a mysterious personal element that cannot be understood and, on the other hand, a quality that may be tested for and taught to anyone. The combination of these views leads to "group-think," where someone responsible for action says, "I will select creative people, but since creativity is so mysterious and unpredictable, I may have missed on some, so I will put several together and hope for the best."

The personal-mystery view of creative experience implies the absolute uniqueness of the individual. For the last century this view has dominated autobiographical reports of creative experience as well as biographical interpretations. Preoccupation with the personal-mystery view of creative process severely hampers a study of the creative process. The individual who records, after the fact, his own creative experience is a questionable source of accurate data, since his understandable tendency will be to bury the nature of his actual experience under an avalanche of egocentric subjectivity. Similarly, the biographer must be doubted, since his identification with his subject leads him to dramatize the importance of individual genius, of personalized, mystic experience, at the expense of objective analysis of the complex interplay between the individual and the world around the "hero." For instance, Edison, during his productive years, collected around himself a working group whose members complemented and stimulated his individual abilities.[1] The biographer, entangled in his identification with the individual genius of an Edison, distorts and minimizes the group in order to nourish his heroic image.

This emphasis on individual genius is reflected in another way by total reliance on the fiction of moments of insight, as though such moments were isolated from high-energy output and coherent work process. Not only the romanticizing biographer, but also the individual artist-scientist himself, reports creative experience in terms of inexplicable insight, neglecting the workaday routine that has given the insight an underpinning.[2] At the opposite pole, overemphasis on "group" as an ultimate creative context can be equally detrimental whether we call the group a team, a task force, or a committee. The group, without a disciplined, integrated approach, degenerates toward its lowest common denominator, i.e., toward the level of the "safest," the most obvious, and most superficial. The group in this sense deserves all the criticism presently being leveled at group-think.[3] The hopeful assumption which seems to underlie the most naive group-think activity is that minds and/or abilities are quantitatively additive—that three individuals with I.Q.'s of 50 equal one with an I.Q. of 150, or that three moderately creative individuals are equal to one highly creative individual. A corollary to this view about group work is: "If A does not think of a solution, B or C will." And if no solution is reached, the blame can be comfortably spread.

This dilemma can be resolved both philosophically and practi-

[1] Nerney, Mary Childs, *Thomas A. Edison: A Modern Olympian* (New York: Harrison Smith & Robert Haas, 1934), pp. 60–68, 159, 217.

[2] Poincaré is an exception. He was aware of the tremendous amount of effort and concentration which underlies any moment of insight. Poincaré, Henri, *Science and Method,* translated by Francis Maitland (New York: Dover Publications, Inc., 1952), pp. 52–63.

[3] Results of Yale Study, conducted by Professor Donald W. Taylor of Yale University, released 1958.

cally. On a philosophical level the resolution involves two parallel recognitions: 1) that the human individual is always in search of his uniqueness; and 2) that he is always committed to membership in some kind of group; the individual grows not unidirectionally (from group-family to individual-unique), but by a continuing oscillation between two poles. On a practical, functioning level the resolution entails two steps: 1) every member of the group must be personally committed to getting the problem solved in the best possible way; 2) in this frame of mind it is possible for members of the group to oscillate between an emphasis on the individual and his personal capabilities (A: "I need the best solution and maybe B has a better idea than I have."), and emphasis on the group and its collective capabilities (B: "With their help I may get a better solution than I could get alone."). The operations of working Synectics groups have demonstrated that the above mentioned conflict can be resolved.[4]

Throughout our research into the creative process, observation of Synectics groups at work in seminars and as individuals building models has revealed the insights. The psychological states and mechanisms that occur when an individual creates are normally underground. The Synectics group situation, which forces each participant to verbalize his thoughts and feelings about the problem at hand, can bring elements of the process out in the open where they can be identified and analyzed.

We have found that for problem solving, as well as for the purpose of research into creative process, a properly operating group has advantages over an individual. Indeed, a Synectics group can compress into a few hours the kind of semi-conscious mental activity which might take months of incubation for a single person. This "efficient" use of the subconscious leads to our insights. This phenomenon, which happens repeatedly when a well trained group is operating smoothly, depends on members of Synectics groups being willing to function on a more or less non-rational basis. In other

---

[4] Gordon, William J. J.: "Operational Approach to Creativity," *Harvard Business Review*, Vol. 34, November–December (1956), No. 6, pp. 41–49.

words, they must avoid trying always to express rational completed concepts. The seamless sphericity of a "closed loop" thought presents an idea association in the impregnable form of a perfectly smooth surface. When an idea is expressed after being completely worked out it is either acceptable as true or unacceptable as untrue. It resists modification. It lives or dies as uttered. No one else can find his way in and build on it; the author of the thought finds himself adorned with a conceptual jewel which is isolated and untouchable. Non-rational communication, on the other hand, produces evocative metaphors, images with rough surfaces, and fissures on which others can get a grip and participate. Of course, this kind of non-rational interplay is only part of a process which spirals up toward increasing coherence. Ultimate solutions to problems are rational; the process of finding them is not.

Another advantage of the group situation is its effect upon individual daring.[5] To achieve radical new approaches to old problems it is essential to take "psychological chances," to abandon familiar ways of looking at things, even to transcend one's image of oneself. A can say, "I feel like defying the law of gravity now." Taken literally, this is a hair-raising announcement. But A has confidence that the group will interpret him figuratively, sensitive to his sudden vague desire to fly in the face of accepted physics. It does not attend so much to the exact implication of his statement as to its motivation. It wants to help him. His predicament arouses it. The risk he has taken has psychological prestige for the group, as though he had launched himself on a dangerous mission.

The backgrounds of the individuals who have made up the central Synectics group in Cambridge during the last few years have been enormously varied. Before there was any attempt to establish other Synectics groups, membership in the central organization shifted to include various combinations of painters, sculptors, mathematicians, advertising men, physicists, philosophers, chemists, actors,

[5] Gordon, William J. J.: "Some Environmental Aspects of Creativity" paper delivered to the Department of Defense, Fort Belvoir, Va., December 1955.

mechanical engineers, architects, electrical engineers, marketing men, chemical engineers, sociologists, biologists, physiologists, musicians, anthropologists, and zoologists. These changes in personnel were part of the experiment; they were not planned to meet particular invention requirements. The purpose was to integrate into a Synectics group people of opposing personality and differing academic background. The most elegant solution to a given problem is one where the solution is the simplest in proportion to the complexity of the variables involved. In other words, the following equation holds:

$$elegance\ of\ solution = \frac{multiplicity\ of\ variables}{simplicity\ of\ solution}\ .$$

The multiplicity factor is represented by the number and diversity of members of a Synectics group. The simplicity factor, hopefully, would result from the application of Synectics theory toward unifying participants and concepts. Our hypothesis was that a general level of novelty (as opposed to marginal improvements) depends on the widest variety of skill, knowledge, and interest being brought to bear. Obviously the problem was to draw interaction and constructive communication from people whose difficulty in understanding each other could lead to mistrust. This interaction was brought about by the mechanisms which make up a methodology common to all areas of creative thought and which can be used to unify the most widely diverse groups.

A further advantage of the shifting diversity of personnel within the group was to bring a wide range of response, both positive and aberrant, to the methods and discipline which we were attempting to evolve. In our experience to date, the most important criterion for the selection of new members for a given group is emotional constitution as against intellectual background. "Emotional constitution" refers to the way a person attacks a problem: (a) Does he thunder in or circle around? (b) In the face of apparent defeat is he passive or does he aggressively strive for success? (c) Is he amused or self-protective when he's been wrong? (d) Can he use his conceptual energy effectively or does he tire at critical junctures? In this sense, the Synectics group differs from the "task force" since the task force approach implies a group of technical experts picked with a given problem (and its assumed area of solution) in mind. In the selection of personnel for Synectics activity, if we are faced with a choice between two individuals of different intellectual backgrounds, but of similar emotional orientations, our tendency would be to choose only one. On the other hand, two individuals having the same intellectual background but different emotional patterns of response could be included in an integrated group which is designed to reflect extreme diversity.

A single way of questioning experience and the phenomena surrounding it leads to a narrow range of answers. True emotional and experiential diversity permits the group not only to tolerate several question-approaches at the same time, but also to probe in depth along any one of the question-lines. Thus, a problem which traditionally suggests a question and an answer derived from chemistry may well be approached and solved from microbiology as a "new point of departure." For example, one Synectics group was given the responsibility for inventing a radically new product in the area of paints and finishes. Made up of a zoologist as well as a physicist, a biologist as well as a chemist, an artist as well as an engineer, the group did not limit itself to paint chemistry. Instead, it directed its thoughts to an organic covering, which led to the notion of "organic paint" made up of seed forms of primitive plants such as lichens, algae and mosses. These tiny soredia (spores) can be "canned" in a nutrient adhesive solution so that they will stay on a wall and grow there.

Naturally, no single group of from five to seven people can embrace technical competence in all areas of science. Therefore, when an examination of feasibility is necessary, we may introduce into the group an expert in a given field. The expert plays the role either of encyclopedia or devil's advocate. As encyclopedia he becomes an automatic knowledge box; if punched in the right place, he responds with the proper technical advice. As devil's advocate he isolates the areas of weakness in a given concept. In some cases the outside expert who has been called in on a specific job becomes a long term, irregular member of the group. He becomes interested in the group's method and its potential, and learns to work like a regular member. To do this he transforms the terminology of his own specialty into language all of the group can understand. He must be willing to invade, as a talented amateur, the fields of other experts as well as to accept the group's invasion of his own field.

The most important (and most underrated) single aspect of a Synectics project is the implementation (in the form of working models) of those concepts developed as solutions. Such model building is vital to the success of a new product or invention program. Moreover, we have observed that unless a teaching program includes the experience of "getting the hands dirty" by actively implementing conceptions, the program is threatened with incompletion and impotence precisely because it is limited to over-abstract discussion.[6] Abstraction breeds more abstraction and more generality instead of leading to tough yes-no tests. Without the pragmatic "does-it-work?" criterion which can be demanded of something reduced to practice, it is impossible to get the specificity and concreteness necessary to the evolution and proof of principle.

A corollary to the experience of implementation is the pragmatic criterion derived. How better judge the *effectiveness* of Synectics theory than by the value of the "hardware" it produces? When we discover what we think is another insight into creative process, we define it operationally. If, in use, it leads to repeated breakthroughs, we call our operational definition a mechanism. As a mechanism we test it with other Synectics groups to make certain it isn't merely a superficial accidental aspect of our own operation. If it continues to lead to new concepts and these concepts lead to successful working

[6] Actual laboratory implementation involves working out solutions to the specific problems which arise in reduction to practice. These solutions are as important as the original concept, but concepts have more prestige in our culture because conceptualizers usually attain the status of administrators, and administrators keep their suitcoats on; they don't build working models.

models, then we accept the mechanism's validity as being proved. (See page 33 for description of psychological mechanisms.)

THE GROWTH OF SYNECTICS THEORY

It may be helpful in the understanding of Synectics to outline briefly the history of our research into the nature of the creative process. There already exists material which deals with the creative motivation and results of the creative process, particularly in the area of esthetics. Our research has been more experientially grounded, although we read and studied in the general area of esthetics before starting our experiments in 1944. We decided to attack the mystery of creative process exactly where the literature stopped, namely, at an operational description of the creative process itself.

In 1944 we began a series of observations of an individual who was involved simultaneously in the processes of psychoanalysis and invention. The result of this state was a double consciousness on the inventor's part: he combined the ability to be aware of the mental process in himself at the same time that he worked with the process toward intention-goal. The inventor who was the subject of these initial researches was presented by the government with a problem in instrumentation. Many accidents to aircraft had occurred as a result of misreading instruments with dial faces.[7] Most of these reading errors arose from the fact that the eye is confused by two revolving motions which require an interpolated reading (cf. Fig. 1). But the eye is rarely deceived when one of the measurements is on a dial and the other is on a band (cf. Fig. 2). Traditional research had produced a mechanical mare's nest of interlocking selsyns, little gears, and wheels in an attempt to produce an instrument having the reading advantages of the second example (cf. Fig. 3). But the psychological problem involving the eye's ability to read and interpolate was further complicated by the presence of mechanical error due to friction.

[7] Gordon, William J. J., "The Integration of Creative Persons," paper delivered to Sloan Fellows, M.I.T., November, 1952.

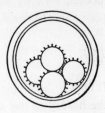

Figure 1   Figure 2   Figure 3

The problem confronting our subject was to devise a dial which would abolish both the psychological reading error and the mechanical friction error. As he worked on this dual problem he made notes and talked into wire recorders and dictaphones in an attempt to produce a live record of his process. On the one hand he was actually solving the problem; on the other hand he was trying to describe the psychological states which seemed to characterize the various phases of his solution. The following are some excerpts from his records:

". . . I am taking apart this airplane altimeter. Why! There must be over a hundred little gears in this mess . . . I notice that springs are essential. I can imagine throwing out any other element but this master spring . . . this foundation spring. Any isolated unit for measuring altitude by pressure will have to be backed up somehow by one or more springs. . . . Thinking about springs, I find that I feel very much removed . . . sort of cut off from the unit I'm playing with, even though it's right in front of me. . . . It seems to be disintegrating almost of its own accord. There are the pieces . . . what piece can I least afford to throw out? The spring is central here . . . but what is the spring? What does it mean to say of a spring that it is a spring? How would I feel if I were a spring? I find myself very mixed up with this spring. I can't get away from my own springiness . . . even if I wanted to. But I don't want to. I am folding in and then expanding, folding in and then expanding . . . or I'm being pulled out and then I'm being pushed back in. Tight! This I don't like. I don't like this tight feeling . . . I don't like this feeling of being pulled way out either. Someone's got me by the hands and the legs, stretching me over a rack, torturing me. . . .

"What if an altimeter just were a spring? . . . No, that couldn't be
. . . . Never mind about altimeters. The same goes for springs anywhere. To hell with getting a quick answer to this problem! I've got to
take a real look . . . from way out. . . . Otherwise I'll just invent
the same thing all over again. . . . What about springs themselves?"

"What's springiness? A spring . . . well, it's like the seasons, in
. . . out, they alternate, in . . . . out. . . . Or, like a mechanical
memory. You can teach a spring to do something by building in some
kind of response . . . even more perfectly than you can train a child
. . . except for hysteresis. I wonder what hysteresis would be in a
child? I'm very sorry, Madam; your child has advanced hysteresis and
we've got to operate immediately. . . .

"Now what is this damn problem? The damn problem is a spring
and an altimeter. It's hard not to think right away about the final solution . . . can't forget about solutions. Solutions are the payoff! But to
hell with them. It's hard to just consider a spring, alone, nothing to do
with anything, just a spring. . . . There on my desk the problem is
printed clearly in that very dark type the government uses to send out
its specifications. In the drawer with it . . . never mind that. . . . Now
if I can get this spring out of here. That's what I want, just get this
spring . . . I'll throw away the rest of the stuff and I'll just look at
the spring. This is a spring now, in front of me. I wind it up and I let
it unwind. I wind it up and I let it unwind . . . of course the most elegant solution would be to have a dial . . . no gears. My God, there
must be two hundred gears in this model! I don't want any gears. That's
of course impossible, but just the same, how can the spring itself do
everything? What *do* I want? I want a spring . . . well, I want it to
run the dial, the outside dial, and of course the real problem is how to
get a band out of this motion. Let me look at the motion again. How
do you get inside that spring? If I . . . if there were an enormous
spring . . . a spring as big as a house, and I hold onto it and it goes
in and out, in and out. What happens to me? Well, let's see, I can put
a little drop of ink on the thing. Now I wind it in and out. Look. If I
get a spring big enough, as the spring tightens . . . the blob of ink will
move in . . . and out as the spring relaxes. . . .

"Funny . . . now I have the feeling that this thing is on its own,
completely outside me . . . that the whole idea is no longer . . . no
longer anything to do with being mine, my idea . . . it's just like fly-
ing now because if I put a spot on the spring and tighten it up, it per-
forms an arc which is exactly the band I'm looking for [cf. Fig 4 (a),
(b), (c)]. It's amazing, and this is no longer I . . . it's as though it

was taken away from me. . . . This must be what people mean when they say you start writing a play and the people you've put in the play just go on by themselves."

(a)   (b)   (c)

Figure 4

While this series of quotations from notes and recorded musings has been edited for continuity, it is a fair representation of the material from which we isolated the key moments, the key states, in our subject's process toward solution. The interrelated psychological states which seemed basic in this narrative were defined as follows:

1a. *Detachment:* The feeling which the inventor described as being "removed . . . sort of cut off. . . . I've got to take a real look . . . from way out. . . ."

1b. *Involvement:* The closeness implied by, "How would I feel if I were a spring? I find myself very mixed up with this spring. I can't get away from my own springiness."

2. *Deferment:* The sense that it was difficult though necessary to discipline himself against premature attempt at solution: "Solutions are the payoff! But to hell with them. . . . Otherwise I'll invent the same thing all over again."

3. *Speculation:* The recurrent ability to let the mind run free: "What happens if an altimeter were just a spring? . . . If there were an enormous spring? . . . I wonder what hysteresis would be in a child?"

4. *Autonomy of Object:* The feeling described at the end of the narrative, as the problem approaches conceptual solu-

tion: "I have the feeling that this thing is on its own, completely outside of me. . . . the people you've put in a play
just go on by themselves."

We observed that these psychological states were present when
the subject effected breakthroughs on the way to his final solution.
Furthermore, it was obvious that the identified states became more
concentrated as he neared his final solution. However, we wanted to
assure ourselves that these psychological states were not merely
symptoms of one man's idiosyncratic subjective response. Therefore, in 1945, following an informal tabulation of the results of the
above research, we initiated a series of interviews with people in art
and science. These interviews at the most formal level consisted of
asking the interviewee whether he had experienced the psychological
states which the inventor in the above experiment had observed and
described. Essentially there were two kinds of response to these
interviews. Some welcomed probing their inner workings unafraid
that this probing would somehow destroy their intuitive capacity.
Introspective interviewees of this kind, who were willing to reply to
the personal queries essential for honest response, immediately
tended to correlate and reinforce the inventor's responses. They said
that the psychological states which the inventor had described were
states that they themselves recognized although they had never been
either aware of nor articulate about them. The other kind of person
interviewed refused to discuss the (to him) mystical workings of his
mind, and it was not for many months that the results and responses
began to come in from the last of those people who, when first interviewed, were highly opposed to introspection.

More than a year later we made a final evaluation and noted a
high degree of correlation between the experiences of both the
highly resistant hold-outs and the more responsive interviewees. At
the time of these interviews there was little or no order of importance given to the recurrent states which were isolated as characteristic of the inventor's psychological processes. A further difficulty
arose from our primitive grasp of the "insights." As a result

all interviewing had to be conducted on a personal basis and responses often appeared to be based on the interviewee's reaction to the personality of the interviewer. After the data from the interviews had been informally tabulated, it was apparent that the four aspects of psychological process [Involvement-Detachment, Deferment, Speculation, and Autonomy of Object (see p. 26)] were universal enough to warrant experimental attempts to feed them back into problem-solving situations. This was attempted at Harvard Underwater Sound Laboratories with groups working on problems in hydrodynamics and acoustics. However, our understanding of the different psychological states was too naive to permit us to feed them back into the groups with experimental clarity, and the success of these experiments was marginal for several reasons:

1. Attempts to "feed back" tended to freeze the working groups because individuals became self-conscious. When we would say, "Let's become more involved here. . . ," or "Can't we defer from an immediate solution for a while?" we met with formidable resistance. The groups not only resented the attempt being made to manipulate them, but they were angered by what they considered irrelevant frivolity. From time to time an individual would rise up and take our bait as though it were perfectly natural for him to think along the lines we were trying to introduce. This kept up our spirits, but in every instance the pressure of the remainder of the group with its emphasis on "Tough-minded engineering will take care of this problem" pulled away the whole group's approach from our influence.

2. In each group there was at least one egocentric who could have been controlled only by an unpermissible degree of authority on the part of the person seeking to conduct these group sessions. Often a group initially would show some enthusiasm for experimenting with the psychological states. This enthusiasm, however, was an easy mark for any individual who established himself as the "conscience" of the group by implying that our experiment flew in the face of the scientific

method. This "conscience" person would state or insinuate that he and his technical associates had not been awarded their Ph.D.'s to be told that they had wasted their time—that there was a short cut to scientific discovery. This aggressive kind of self-protection we found impossible to combat with the feeble tools at our disposal.

3. Since these first sessions were not recorded, it was difficult to analyze failure or to improve technique. It was impossible to remember the statements and specific attitudes of resistance to our experiments. Therefore, it did not become clear to us that the psychological states were too abstract in the form we were using them. Also, it was not obvious that we had made a major mistake by introducing them philosophically rather than personally. For instance, if we felt that involvement was the state which would be most constructive in a given situation we would say, "Let's try to involve ourselves with this problem . . . to identify with it." We should have said, "I find myself right inside this problem. My ears and eyes and arms are elements of it." We now know that if we had used the latter approach the groups would have respected our willingness to "risk" involvement and the chances of their participation would have been vastly increased.

Though the information derived from the above experiment was limited, the experience did teach us one important thing about directing our future research into creative process. Previously we had aimed our efforts toward understanding what occurred in the human mind at the exact time of discovery. After these informal experiments at Harvard Underwater Sound Laboratory, we shifted the focus of our research to attempt to understand the psychological conditions and mental states which characterize the creative process as a whole. Our new objective was to achieve a knowledge which would enable us to increase measurably the probability of inventive breakthrough. We did not abandon our initial desire to define the moment of breakthrough itself; we pushed that goal into the background temporarily while we tried to be more exact about the psychological conditions which characterized the whole process of invention.

Shortly after these interviews were completed, our research took the form of an increasing interest in the similarity of the creative process in art with that in science—a similarity which was made quite apparent by the response of both artists and scientists to the interviews. The Rock Pool Experiment was established in 1948. This experiment involved settling a group of between twelve and twenty artists (some with, and some without, families) in Lisbon, New Hampshire, for the summer months. The purpose of this center was to supply a climate in which artists of various types could live together and trade ideas, through both conversation and observation, of the growth and development of each other's work. The living together involved not only sociological disciplines but also technical ones, in the sense that the artists were responsible for building houses, installing and repairing plumbing, etc. It was hoped that a group of esthetically oriented individuals would reveal mechanisms of creative process which were more concrete than the psychological states. We had confidence that new insights could be gained from observing the processes of artists because in the course of our series of interviews we found that artists in general were more articulate than technical people about their subconscious or subjective mental activity.

In the course of the experiment, members of the Rock Pool group won many prizes, including the Tiffany prize for painting, several graphic arts prizes, and numerous awards for silver work, sculpture, and ceramics. All but one of the members of the group have gone on with careers in the arts and have become well known in their respective fields. (This does not mean, of course, that the Rock Pool Experiment was the direct cause of the success of the participating artists.) However, it became apparent that the attempt to test and evolve a working concept of the nature of the creative process in the esthetic situation was not as productive of data and of eventual results as a similar attempt in a more technically (scientifically) oriented group might be.

The Rock Pool Experiment exposed no new insight into creative process but it did disclose a significant procedure for implementing the research itself, i.e., the use of the group, as opposed to an individual, as the tool to capture further slippery elements of the subtle procedure of inventive activity. The recurrent group gatherings at Rock Pool were directed toward the solution to a variety of problems. The participating members of this job-oriented group were sufficiently unself-protective to communicate through shorthand free associations. In the case of our first research subject who was working alone (see p. 15) our insights were limited to his best efforts to record his underlying subjective musings while attempting to solve an objective problem. In the group problem-solving situation at Rock Pool, it was apparent that some psychological undertones of creative process, imperceptible till then, were discernible. When a creative person is "talking to himself" he does not have to talk out loud, but in a group situation where individuals believe that elegance of solution depends on contributed communication— they talk out loud. Thus certain nuances of the mechanism of creative process began to be revealed. And from this time on the invention group became the major tool for increasing our knowledge and making it concrete. By reviewing tapes of sessions where conceptual breakthroughs were achieved, we were able, slowly and painstakingly, to isolate increasingly clear, recurrent patterns of mental activity which accompanied the creative process.

In conjunction with experiments in vivo using taped sessions, the researches into creative process undertaken in Cambridge, in 1944, involved a study of the classical works in the field: Groos, Freud, Lange, Bosanquet, Aristotle, James; and a study of autobiographical records such as those of Einstein, Goethe, Coleridge, Kipling, Edison, Wordsworth, Poincaré, and others. In 1949, although we did not expect to find additional material which would be of direct assistance to us, we felt obliged to reopen our researches into the literature. With the classical and autobiographical studies behind us, our intention was to review all available information on contemporary research. We were disappointed to learn that most of the modern studies of the creative process were attempts to devise test methods of identifying creative people. These studies were of little help to us since they were on the one hand, related to "test" for creativity and, on the other hand, related to a theory about creativity which (a) outlined the conditions of the test, and then (b) measured itself by the results of the test. There could be but one measure of the results of a research program devoted to Synectics investigation of the creative process, namely, the end product.

Thus, our efforts to derive usable data from *artistic activity* were shifted in favor of a study of the invention process in *technology*. This was in no way an abandonment of the arts as a field for further study, but a researcher's choice, made on the assumption that the creative process in art and in science is essentially the same. The choice was modified by the further assumption that the process might be more easily evaluated in science. Technical invention, while every bit as subjective in process as artistic creation, is not exposed to an equally subjective evaluation of the end product, presupposing the definition "it works or it doesn't work" as the measure of inventive success.

At this time we also reviewed, in a formal academic way, the analyses of the creative process which were available to us in the literature of art, philosophy, psychology, science, and autobiography. We were disturbed to note that the statements made by psychologists and philosophers lean toward abstraction and over-objectivity.[8] Psychological states—the human mind, emotion, and imagination—are treated as generalities. These analyses are not invalid, but their very generality and objectivity (this, then, is the nature of man) divorces analysis from concrete experience. While this literature may serve

[8] With the exception of "psychical distance" as discussed by Edward Bullough in "Psychical Distance as a Factor in Art and Aesthetic Principle," *British Journal of Psychology* V (1912–13) pp. 87–118, and "esthetic distance" as formulated by José Ortega y Gasset in *The Dehumanization of Art.* (tr. Helene Weyl) Princeton: Princeton University Press, 1948.

as a useful guide, it provides little direct help for defining creativity in operational and repeatable terms. Autobiographical description of the process, as experienced, is usually over-subjective and after-the-fact. Although poetic and in itself suggestive, it is more elusive than workable analysis of the process it intends to describe.

At the conclusion of this period of research we committed ourselves to produce descriptions and definitions directly related to the experience of the creative process itself. Our purpose was to develop a scheme which individuals could understand and use to increase the probability of their creative success. Our task was to isolate psychological mechanisms and to record recurrent psychological states which could be described in concrete terms and learned in an experimental (not primarily a theoretical) sense. For example, while we accepted Freud's notion of regression and its role in the creative process as a valid notion, it seemed impossible to teach people to regress; therefore Freud's insight was of little operational use to us.[9] We were forced to interpret the theory of regression in functional terms.

The next step in the research was the formation in 1952 of an operating group at Arthur D. Little, Inc., in Cambridge, Massachusetts. The first integrated group devoted to technological invention was responsible for producing invention results. No attempt was made at this time to establish other Synectics groups. This group was composed of: a physicist with interest in psychology; an electromechanical engineer; an anthropologist with interest in electronics; a graphic artist with the added background of industrial engineering; and a sculptor with some background in chemistry. (The last two were drawn from personnel involved in the Rock Pool Experiment.) At the beginning of this group's operations, introspective observation of process and inquiry into themes and mechanisms was kept at a minimum. The reason for this was an anxiety concerning the group's ability to be, on the one hand, involved in the process of invention and, on the other, detached and observant of the process

[9] Kris, Ernst, *Psychoanalytic Exploration in Art* (New York: International Universities Press, 1952).

—without inhibiting the capacity to produce creatively. It became increasingly clear that the psychological states were still far from reliable as operational tools. The concept of these psychological states evolved into that of operational mechanisms between the years of 1953 and 1959. This advance in technique was a consequence of the group's style of working through conversation and discussion. All Synectics sessions were—and still are—tape recorded.[10] By listening to tapes of productive sessions it was possible to unmask recurrent conditions, states, and mechanisms which previously had gone unnoticed except in the most vaguely subjective and intuitive sense. At this point it became necessary to seek the assistance of people who could achieve the dual role of inventing while examining the process of invention for two reasons: (1) to avoid a hypothesis which was based on a singular subjective intuition; and (2) to identify more concretely the elements of the process.

The members of this group shifted. To date more than thirty people have participated in the primary Synectics group; yet the group has never had more than six or seven members at one time. It is our conviction that few people (and this holds for members of the group itself) are able to tolerate the psychological discipline of observing themselves over a long period of time. The philosophical-psychological estheticians who hold that it is impossible to be at the same time in the creative process and aware of process are wrong; but it is indeed difficult.

From this point the pattern of theory and hypothesis began to mature rapidly. The recurrent psychological states, identified and defined in 1945 (Involvement-Detachment, Deferment, Speculation, and Autonomy of Object) became more plastic, more manageable in an operational context. The psychological states grew increasingly useful as they drew closer to being operational mechanisms. These mechanisms are concrete functional tools for taking advantage of

---

[10] These tapes serve three functions: (a) review of tapes is a powerful training tool allowing group members to criticize their Synectics technique; (b) in the excitement of a session valuable viewpoints may be buried, to be revealed in a more leisurely audit when participants are not so involved; (c) tapes are a legal record of conceptual priority.

the insights implied by the valid but abstract theoretical psychological states. In 1956 other recurrent states and mechanisms were identified and to a degree defined. For instance, we noticed a recurrent reliance on the "commonplace" as a point of creative departure. By "commonplace," in the first attempts to define its use, we understood those vast areas of everyday experience which are elementary or obvious to the sophisticated technical mind. For instance, from thinking of commonplace summer night insects came a theory for acoustical insect control; from remembering the commonplace action of fish responding to an underwater sound came the theory of how to drive fish so as to catch them without nets.

We spent considerable time during 1956 in an attempt to define the role of the leader in the Synectics group: to what degree did he have to enjoy a teacher's authority? Reviews of tapes showed that while the group had an identifiable administrative leader, the role of intellectual leader shifted from person to person in the course of a series of sessions. Tentatively, we concluded that a strong leader caused the group (in session and out) to try to second-guess him or strive to win his approval. In short, and contrary to the usual assumption, it was desirable in the Synectics group to have too many chiefs and not enough Indians. (However, today we believe that either the strong leader or multiple leader approach can be successful.)

In 1956, following a lengthy investigation of Synectics research covering the years since 1946, the Rockefeller Foundation gave a grant to Harvard University for the purpose of bringing academic psychology into immediate contact with our efforts. Professor Jerome Bruner and Dr. Jean Pool worked with us for many months, actually participating in a series of sessions devoted to the solution of a particular problem. Thanks to Professor Bruner's suggestion, it was during this period (1956–1957) that we began to distinguish formally between the recurrent psychological states and the mechanisms (operational methods of initiating and sustaining those states).

In 1958 we noticed that, in launching a series of sessions which culminated in the successful solution of a given problem, we were constantly attempting to "make the familiar strange." Faced with the all too familiar, without understanding entirely what we were doing, we would attempt at first radically to shift our vision so that the familiar (the codified, the set world of the usual) was made strange and new, and therefore subject to new patterns and new laws of operation—subject to invention. Once we had identified this activity we used it consciously, asking: "How can we 'make the familiar strange' here?"

Initial success with this technique led us to extend it, to consider various ways of making the familiar strange. After the practice of seeking and sustaining an analogy was noted on the tapes, it was tested by the use of conscious mechanisms, and it rendered exciting results. Various forms of analogy, subsequently superseded by the more inclusive concept of metaphor, became the Synectics operational mechanisms. All the Synectics groups (within as well as outside the parent group) had shown a recurrent tendency to identify, as the altimeter inventor did when he asked himself: "What would I feel like if I were a spring?" "How would a spring feel if it were human?" We deliberately fed this tendency back into group sessions, and since its use led to successful solutions we concluded that this was one mechanism for initiating and sustaining inventive effort. This particular mechanism was injected by persuading participants to imagine how they would feel if they were the inanimate elements of the problem under consideration. For instance, in a session devoted to the invention of an unbreakable yet translucent plastic glass the group was encouraged to describe their subjective response at "being" an actual piece of glass. How did they feel? Which way were they pulled? Did they want to stay close to their brother particles?

When the goal of invention is achieved, it is preceded, signalled, and accompanied by a pleasurable mental excitement. This pleasurable excitement itself (the feeling of being on the right track) is a purposeful psychological state, recognized unconsciously as an indicator of the direction to take. The ability to hunt for and to recognize this pleasurable-pragmatic excitement traditionally has been labelled as accidental and intuitive. However, it is our conclusion that this pleasure-sense of direction is purposeful and is a psychological state subject to cultivation as a skill in pursuit of the successful climax of the inventive process. We observed that certain people repeatedly selected ways of thinking about a problem which led to elegant solutions. These people confessed to a pleasurable feeling—a feeling of "being on the track"—long before their intuition was proved correct. They said that they regarded this pleasurable feeling as a signal telling them they were headed in the right direction. Our technique used the tape recordings of sessions to teach people to look for this pleasurable feeling in themselves and act on it. When A had made an intuitive breakthrough, we would play the tape back for A to recall how he felt at the time he was aware of it. Or we would have A describe the sensation to B so that B would be on the lookout for it in himself.

During 1957 reviews of tapes, together with closer observations and questions of individuals, suggested another pair of psychological conditions necessary for successful inventive effort. We noticed that the ability to tolerate and use the irrelevant was of fundamental importance for a solution. By the irrelevant we understand attitudes, information, and observations which, from a common-sensical and (more often) from a technical point of view, do not seem relevant to the problem under consideration. As a companion state, the ability to play, to sustain a childlike willingness to suspend adult disbelief, emerged as a psychological condition of making the familiar strange. However, words like "play" and "irrelevant" are operationally meaningless, and in 1958–59 we turned our attention from a study of recurrent psychological states and the conditions which support them to a further study of those mechanisms which would help us to make the familiar strange. We reviewed and analyzed tapes of sessions which had contributed to successful invention projects; and then those mechanisms which we could isolate and partially define we used and observed in both invention and teaching sessions. Three general types of mechanisms for play have emerged from these studies: (1) play with words, with meanings and definitions; (2) play in pushing a fundamental law or a basic scientific concept "out of phase"; and (3) play with metaphor.

Play with words, meanings, and definitions involves transposing a specific invention problem into a general word or a general statement. Thus, in one Synectics group an assignment to invent a radically new can opener began with a three hour session which was sustained play with the word "open." We also included "inversion" in this mechanism as another method of play with accepted meanings. Thus, while we usually assume that a large magnet draws to it a piece of iron we can invert and say that the piece of iron has hunted for and found a place to go. In a small way we have made the familiar strange because we have shifted our concentration from the persuasive female lodestone to the aggressive little piece of male iron.

The effort to push a law or a concept out of phase can range from postulating a universe in which water does run uphill (in order to approach a problem in hydrodynamics) to asking: "How can we really deny or repeal the second and third laws of thermodynamics?" Or: "How can we *apparently* deny entropy?" Recently we have used this mechanism with invention success by simply concentrating on the question: "What law shall we choose to push out of phase?" or, granted a given invention problem: "What law would it be most appropriate or advantageous to upset?"

Play with metaphor is one of the most fruitful of the mechanisms which can be used to make the familiar strange. We have experimented with metaphors which involve expressed or implied comparisons between relatively "like" things or states: "Wiring a building should be like plumbing," as well as with metaphors which have the shock value of comparing unlike things or unlike states: "For humans 'absence makes the heart grow fonder.' Essentially, this is in conflict with the inverse square law." As a special extension of metaphor we make considerable conscious use of analogy, i.e., comparisons between things with like functions and different forms. Personification and anthropomorphization fit here with the question:

"How would it feel if it were human and could feel?" "How would I feel if I were it?" As a further special case of feeling as an inanimate object would feel, we have experimented successfully with attempts to empathize, to feel, kinesthetically, in interrelation of the muscles themselves, the state of an inanimate object, a motion, or a relationship.

Exciting as it is for Synectics groups to succeed in making the familiar strange, it is hardly an end in itself. The end is a functioning, working model of the invention product, just as the end result of a narrative idea is not the idea but the novel into which it is transformed, or as the end result of a visual insight is the painting into which it is evolved.

Our method of study has not changed appreciably. We have formal group sessions aimed at problem-identification, and problem-solving. These sessions produce concepts which are criticized, researched, and implemented. Obstructions arising in the implementation phases lead to short informal sessions. When a formidable block stands in the way then formal sessions are brought to bear. Experts are used in the fashion described above, although each Synectics group seems to be increasingly efficient in their use, less disturbed by the expert's chronic negativity, and less defensive about its (the group's) own freedom from expert dogma. Tapes are made of formal sessions and are reviewed (a) for the purpose of examining our work process, and (b) as a source of new insights into the invention problems to be solved.

When the Cambridge Synectics group extended its research from its own limited operation to establishing and training groups in other contexts, this proved to be a productive method of data collection. Teaching and training a great variety of people our method of operation forces us to be articulate. We might otherwise leave our working conclusions buried in the private language which is inevitably developed as a shorthand communication among ourselves. Also the reactions of our students and their reformulations of many of our hypotheses have helped to pry us loose from any dogma which we may have developed.

When we established Synectics groups in industries (first in 1955), we were faced with the problem of personnel selection. Here again we reviewed the published material on the subject and the systems which were being applied. But none of these was experiential or concrete enough for us. Therefore, we developed our own approach based on the mechanisms of Synectics theory. We devised an interview program based on searching for individuals who have natural ability to use the mechanisms or who have the capacity to learn to use them. (Chapter 5 is devoted to an analysis and description of this technique.)

The substance of what follows in this book is an attempt to describe the creative process as we see and experience it. I shall try to define the recurrent states which we have identified and to make clear how even an insight into these is not sufficient; it is necessary to translate the theoretical psychological states into the functional mechanisms with operational meaning for students, so they can put into practice the theories implied. Even though the mechanisms are concrete they too must be learned through practice. It is one thing to attain a theoretical grasp of these mechanisms and another matter to absorb them into one's natural *modus operandi*. At first, students are self-conscious in their use of the mechanisms but in time they become spontaneous. Even in the self-conscious stage, however, the mechanisms are effective. Above all, the theories comprised in Synectics are proposed here as hypotheses designed to increase the probability of success in creative activity. The major effective components of creative process are subconscious; so that creative solutions to problems traditionally contain a high "accident" quotient. It is difficult purposely to repeat a process which is only subconsciously perceived. Synectics attempts to make explicitly conscious some of these subconscious mechanisms so that they can be evoked when the need arises.

Synectics defines creative process as the mental activity in problem-stating, problem-solving situations where artistic or technical inventions are the result. I use the expression "problem-stating, problem-solving" rather than merely "problem-solving" in order to include the definition and understanding of the problem. The operational mechanisms of Synectics are the concrete psychological factors which support and press forward creative process. The mechanisms do not pertain to the motivations for creative activity, nor are they intended to be used to judge the ultimate product of an esthetic or technical invention. Psychological states such as empathy, involvement, play, detachment, and use of irrelevance are (as we have seen) basic to creative process but they are not operational. The Synectics mechanisms are intended to induce appropriate psychological states and thus promote creative activity.

Words like intuition, empathy, and play are merely names put to complex activities in the hope that the naming of the activity will in fact describe it. Experience has shown it to be most difficult to feed back into a problem-stating, problem-solving situation such nominalistic abstractions. When dealing with an individual or a group faced with problem-stating and problem-solving, it is ineffectual to attempt to persuade the individual to be intuitive, to empathize, to become involved, to be detached, to play, or to tolerate apparent irrelevance. However, in our research experience the Synectics mechanisms effectively increase the probability of success when creativity is called for. They draw the individual into the psychological states.

The Synectic process involves:

(i) making the strange familiar;
(ii) making the familiar strange.

Making the strange familiar: In any problem-stating, problem-solving situation, the first responsibility of individuals involved is to understand the problem. This is essentially an analytical phase where the ramifications and the fundamentals of the problem must be plumbed. However, if only this analytical step is taken, no novel solution is possible. For work on a problem to get started, some concrete assumptions must be made, although in the course of the problem-stating, problem-solving process, the understanding of the problem may change. It is the function of the mind, when presented with a problem, to attempt to make the strange familiar by means of analysis. The human organism is basically conservative, and any strange thing or concept is threatening to it. When faced with strangeness the mind attempts to engorge this strangeness by forcing it into an acceptable pattern or changing its (the mind's) private geometry of bias to make room for the strangeness. The mind compares the given strangeness with data previously known and in terms of these data converts the strangeness into familiarity.

This is, of course, an obvious part of problem-solving. However, Synectics is an attempt to describe those conscious, preconscious and subconscious psychological states which are present in any creative act. Therefore, it would be an omission not to mention the analytical, the making-the-strange-familiar mechanism. The great pitfall, the traditional danger, in making the strange familiar is in becoming so buried in analysis and detail that these become ends in themselves, leading nowhere. The process of making the strange familiar, if used alone, yields a variety of superficial solutions; but basic novelty demands a fresh viewpoint, a new way of looking at the problem. Most problems are not new. The challenge is to view the problem in a new way. This new viewpoint in turn embodies the potential for a new basic solution.

Making the familiar strange: To make the familiar strange is to distort, invert, or transpose the everyday ways of looking and responding which render the world a secure and familiar place. This pursuit of strangeness is not a blasé's search for the bizarre and out-of-the-way. It is the conscious attempt to achieve a new look at the same old world, people, ideas, feelings, and things. In the "familiar world" objects are always right-side-up; the child who bends and peers at the world from between his legs is experimenting with the familiar made strange. (One sees the familiar tree as a collection of solids in an otherwise empty space. The sculptor consciously may invert his world and see the tree as a series of voids or holes carved within the solid block of the air.)

Owen Barfield quotes a South Sea Islander's pigeon-English description of a three-masted, screw steamer with two funnels: "Thlee-pieces bamboo, two-pieces puff-puff, walk-along inside, no-can-see."[1] In our terms, the conceptions which frame the steamship are firmly established in the realm of the familiar. Here, the familiar Western concept of steamship is juxtaposed with the strange pigeon-English version. Barfield says, "Now when I read the words, 'Thlee-pieces bamboo, two-pieces puff-puff, walk-along inside, no-can-see,' I am for a moment transported into a totally different kind of consciousness. I see the steamer, not from my own eyes, but through the eyes of a primitive South Sea Islander. His experience, his *meaning* is quite different from mine, for it is the product of different concepts. This he reveals by his choice of words; and the result is that, for a moment, I shed Western civilization like an old garment and behold my steamer in a new and strange light."[2] The steamer seen by the Western mind in this light is reconstituted and presented as alive and malleable to the imagination.

These several mechanisms for making the familiar strange are not a collection of mental tricks for the achievement of superficial novelty. They have been developed and are used in the several Synectics groups as a systematic way of solving actual invention problems. Thus, Barfield's "new look" at the familiar steamer could be the starting point for considering propulsion. Combined with technical competence it could in turn lead to a new viewpoint for the development of a new invention.

The attempt to make the familiar strange involves several different methods of achieving an intentionally naive or apparently "out of focus" look at some aspect of the known world. And this look

[1] Barfield, Owen, *Poetic Diction* (London: Faber & Faber, 1957), p 49.
[2] *Ibid.*

can transpose both our usual ways of perceiving and our usual expectations about how we or the world will behave. The experience of sustaining this condition can provoke anxiety and insecurity. But maintaining the familiar as strange is fundamental to disciplined creativity. All problems present themselves to the mind as threats of failure. For someone striving to win in terms of a successful solution, this threat evokes a mass response in which the most immediate superficial solution is clutched frantically as a balm to anxiety. This is consistent with the natural impulse to master the strange by making it familiar. Yet if we are to perceive all the implications and possibilities of the new we must risk at least temporary ambiguity and disorder. Human beings are heir to a legacy of frozen words and ways of perceiving which wrap their world in comfortable familiarity. This protective legacy must be disowned. A new viewpoint depends on the capacity to risk and to understand the mechanisms by which the mind can make tolerable the temporary ambiguity implicit in risking.

Synectics has identified four mechanisms for making the familiar strange, each metaphorical in character:

   (i) Personal Analogy;
   (ii) Direct Analogy;
   (iii) Symbolic Analogy;
   (iv) Fantasy Analogy.

According to our observations, without the presence of these mechanisms no problem-stating, problem-solving attempt will be successful. The mechanisms are to be regarded as specific and reproducible mental processes, tools to initiate the motion of creative process and to sustain and renew that motion. There are romantic and popular prejudices against any such mechanization of human creativity. However, Synectics consciously intends this very mechanization. The mechanisms are thus by definition subject to conscious and deliberate use as primary *means*. In addition, through practice they become habitual as ways of seeing and acting. Even those individuals who by habit unconsciously make use of them have been observed to intensify and heighten their creative effectiveness as a result of the conscious effort to establish and expand the application of these tools.

PERSONAL ANALOGY

Personal identification with the elements of a problem releases the individual from viewing the problem in terms of its previously analyzed elements. A chemist makes a problem familiar to himself through equations combining molecules and the mathematics of phenomenological order. On the other hand, to make a problem strange the chemist may personally identify with the molecules in action. Faraday "looked . . . into the very heart of the electrolyte endeavoring to render the play of its atom visible to his mental eyes."[3] The creative technical person can think himself to be a dancing molecule, discarding the detachment of the expert and throwing himself into the activity of the elements involved. He becomes one of the molecules. He permits himself to be pushed and pulled by the molecular forces. He remains a human being but acts as though he were a molecule. For the moment the rigid formulae don't govern, and he feels what happens to a molecule.

Einstein recognized the role of empathic personalized identification: "The psychical entities which seem to serve as elements in thought are certain signs and more or less clear images which can be 'voluntarily' reproduced and combined . . . this combinatory play seems to be the essential feature in productive thought. . . . The above mentioned elements are, in my case, of visual and some of muscular type."[4] Here a great man of science working in the most abstract area of thought admits "muscular" identifications even with the *a priori* constructs of mathematics. Kekule, by identifying himself with a snake swallowing its tail, developed an insight

[3] Tyndall, John, *Faraday as a Discoverer* (London: Longmans, Green, 1868), pp. 66–67.

[4] Hadamard, Jacques, *The Psychology of Invention in the Mathematical Field* (Princeton: Princeton University Press, 1945), pp. 142–143.

into the benzene molecule in terms of a ring rather than a chain of carbon atoms.[5] Keats describes his writing of *Endymion:* "I leaped headlong into the sea, and thereby have become better acquainted with the sounds, the quicksands, and the rocks, than if I had stayed upon the green shore and piped a silly pipe, and took tea and comfortable advice."[6] Thus, in both science and art, detached observations and analysis are abandoned in favor of Personal Analogy.

Example of Personal Analogy: A Synectics group had been attacking the problem of inventing a new and practical constant speed mechanism: How to run a shaft at speeds varying from four hundred to four thousand rpm so that the power take-off end of this shaft always turns at four hundred. In analyzing the technical elements, the group began to find immediate solutions. As might be imagined all these "solutions too soon" took the form of gears and wheels, cones, or liquid clutches. Since many competent engineers had tried to solve this constant speed problem there was little hope for arriving at anything elegant unless a totally new viewpoint were gained. The mechanism for making this familiar problem strange was Personal Analogy. A sketch was drawn on the blackboard showing a box with a shaft entering and going out. The entering shaft was labelled "400 to 4000"; the exiting shaft was labelled "400 constant." One after the other, each member of the group metaphorically entered the box and attempted without tools to effect with his own body the speed constancy required. Here are some excerpts from the recorded session:

A: Okay I'm in the damn box. I grab the in-shaft with one hand and grab the out-shaft with the other. I let the in-shaft slip when I think it's going too fast so that the out-shaft will stay constant.

B: But how do you know how fast the out-shaft is really going?

A: I read a watch and count.

C: How do you feel in there?

[5] Libby, Walter, "The Scientific Imagination," *Scientific Monthly,* XV (1922), pp. 263–270.
[6] Keats, John, *The Letters of John Keats,* M. Buxton Forman ed. (London: Oxford University Press, 1935), p. 223.

A: Well, my hands are getting . . . too hot to hold I guess . . . at least one hand, that is . . . the one that's acting like a clutch . . . slipping.

C: B, how about you hopping into the box.

B: I see myself in there but I can't do anything because I don't have anything to measure rpm or time . . . I guess I'm in the same spot as A.

C: How about you, D?

D: . . . I'm in the box and I am trying to be a governor . . . to be a feedback system . . . built in. . . . Let's see. If I grab the out-shaft with my hands . . . and let's say there's a plate on the in-shaft so that my feet can press against it. I put my feet way out on the periphery of the plate and . . . what I really would like is for my feet to get smaller as the speed of the in-shaft increases because then the friction would be reduced and I would hold on to the out-shaft for dear life and its speed might remain constant. . . . The faster the in-shaft went the smaller my feet would become so that the driving force would stay the same.

C: How could you get your feet smaller?

A: That's not the way to ask the question . . . better say, "How keep friction constant?"

E: If for some reason, some anti-Newtonian reason, your feet came closer together on the plate as the speed of the in-shaft increases then your leverage would be reduced. . . . I mean that you might keep the resultant force on the out-shaft constant.

C: I kind of go for that "anti-Newtonian" thing . . . we're fighting centrifugal force here.

E: How about a non-Newtonian liquid? . . . a liquid which draws near to the center of rotation instead of being flung out?

B: You'd have an anti-gravity machine.

E: Fine.

A: The only thing that gets closer and closer to the axis of rotation is a string with a weight on the end . . . a string tied to a stick. You twirl the string and it wraps around the stick till it gets shorter and shorter, . . . finally you don't have any string left.

E: How about a liquid made up of many strings . . . or even better an elastic fluid. . . . Listen! Imagine a fluid that's made up of a billion rubber bands. The faster the axis of rotation goes the more the rubber bands wind up on the axis.

C: You'd have to have those rubber bands sticking and unsticking all the time . . . or breaking and unbreaking, wouldn't you?

E: Maybe . . . maybe . . . but it's not nuts. . . .

B: You know what I like about this crazy way to think about this? It's got a built-in governor . . . that's the trouble with present mechanisms. They're hooligans with tachometers and rpm measurers . . . a womb hung round with barking dogs . . . this damn anti-Newtonian liquid would tell itself when to take it easy.

One of the members of the group built a model on this principle. But it was inefficient. It would have been suitable for a sensing device, but not as a power transmitting unit. So the same member built a mechanical analogy of the liquid constant speed device. This model definitely proved the principle and appeared to be efficient and economical.

The mechanism of Personal Analogy is easily understood after exposure to Synectics technique. However, its application demands extensive loss of self. Some individuals habitually are so wed to rigid inner control and rational behaviour that any alternative behaviour is anxiety inducing. To evoke this mechanism the "teacher"[7] sets the example of Personal Analogy (e.g., in above example, he is the first to enter the transfer box) so that the novice loses his fear of loss of control. The novice needs to see what happens to someone else first. Then hesitatingly and finally with relaxed confidence the novice will begin to use the mechanism himself.

DIRECT ANALOGY

This mechanism describes the actual comparison of parallel facts, knowledge, or technology. Sir March Isumbard Brunel solved the

[7] See chapter V for further exposition of the "teacher" role.

problem of underwater construction by watching a shipworm tun-
nelling into a timber. The worm constructed a tube for itself as it
moved forward, and the classical notion of caissons came to Brunel
by Direct Analogy. Hadamard points out, "Especially, biology, as
Hamite used to observe, may be a most useful study even for mathematicians, as hidden but eventually fruitful analogies may appear
between processes in both kinds of study."[8] Albert Einstein observed that "combinatory play seems to be the essential feature in
productive thought."[9] And Alexander Graham Bell recalled, "it
struck me that the bones of the human ear were very massive, indeed, as compared with the delicate thin membrane that operated
them, and the thought occurred that if a membrane so delicate
could move bones relatively so massive, why should not a thicker
and stouter piece of membrane move my piece of steel. And the
telephone was conceived."[10]

Example of Direct Analogy: A Synectics group was faced with
the problem of inventing a dispenser which could be used with
various products from glue to nail polish. The dispenser was to be
in one piece without a top to be removed and replaced with each
use. These specifications meant that the mouth of the dispenser had
to be designed to open for dispensing and to close tightly after use.
Group members directed themselves to a new way of thinking about
the problem. Among the mechanisms which were brought to bear
on the problem was Direct Analogy. The group asked itself what
actions in nature operated the way the dispenser must in order to
satisfy the conditions imposed by the problem.

A: A clam sticks its neck out of its shell . . . brings the neck
back in and closes the shell again.

B: Yeah, but the clam's shell is an exoskeleton. The real part, the
real anatomy of the clam is inside.

C: What difference does that make?

[8] Hadamard, *op. cit.,* p. 9.
[9] Reiser, A., *Albert Einstein* (London: Thornton Butterworth Ltd., 1931),
p. 116.
[10] MacKenzie, Catherine, *Alexander Graham Bell* (New York: Houghton
Mifflin, 1928), pp. 72–73.

A: Well, the neck of the clam doesn't clean itself . . . it just drags itself back into the protection of the shell.

D: What other analogies are there to our problem?

E: How about the human mouth?

B: What does it dispense?

E: Spit . . . the mouth propels spit out whenever it wants . . . oh, oh. It isn't really self cleaning . . . you know, dribbling on the chin.

A: Couldn't there be a mouth which was trained so that it wouldn't dribble?

E: Maybe, but it would be contrived as hell . . . and if the human mouth can't keep itself clean with all the feedback in the human system. . . .

D: When I was a kid I grew up on a farm. I used to drive a hayrack behind a pair of draft horses. When a horse would take a crap, first his outer . . . I guess you'd call it a kind of mouth, would open. Then the anal sphincter would dilate and a horse ball would come out. Afterwards, everything would close up again. The whole picture would be as clean as a whistle.

E: What if the horse had diarrhea?

D: That happened when they got too much grain . . . but the horse would kind of wink a couple of times while the anal mouth was drawn back . . . the winking would squeeze out the liquid . . . then the outer mouth would cover the whole thing up again.

B: You're describing a plastic motion.

D: I guess so . . . could we simulate the horse's ass in plastic?

Later the particular Synectics group working on the dispenser problem built a product which operated almost exactly as described by the above analogy. Diversity of backgrounds among group members provides the richness essential for the successful application of the mechanism of Direct Analogy.

Readings of classical scientific discovery as well as seventeen years of practical invention indicate that a biological perception of physical phenomena produces generative viewpoints. Helmholtz, in discussing the invention of the ophthalmoscope, is clear about the influence of various different scientific fields coming together. "I attribute my subsequent success to the fact that circumstances had fortunately planted me with some knowledge of geometry and training in physics among the doctors, where physiology presented a virgin soil of the utmost fertility, while on the other hand I was led by my acquaintance with the phenomena of life to problems and points of view that are beyond the scope of pure mathematics and physics."[11] The strained comparison of a scientific observation in one field with that of another field tends to force an expression of a problem in a new way. Francis Galton emphasized the necessity for adequate knowledge so that the potentially destructive intrusion of alien ideas can be sifted and matched.[12]

Pasteur writes that his successful work on the dissymmetry of natural organics was based "on varied notions borrowed from diverse branches of science."[13] And Cavendish's habit of "carrying on together, widely dissimilar inquiries"[14] permitted him to be continually comparing the phenomena and theories of one branch of science with those of another. In the arts too we can see the effect of Direct Analogy. For instance, the literature of Goethe was founded in music. He says, "It often seems to me as though an invisible genius were whispering something rhythmical to me, so that on my walks I always keep step to it, and at the same time fancy I hear soft tones accompanying some song."[15] And Schiller states, "With me the conception has at first no definite or clear object: this comes later. A certain musical state of mind precedes it, and this, in me,

[11] Koenigsberger, Leo, *Hermann Von Helmholtz* (Oxford: Clarendon Press, 1906), p. 77.

[12] Galton, Sir Francis, *Inquiries into the Human Faculty and its Development* (London: J. M. Dent & Sons Ltd., 1919).

[13] Vallery-Radot, R., *The Life of Pasteur,* tr. R. L. Devonshire, 2 vols. (Westminster: Archibald Constable & Co., 1902), Vol. I. p. 223.

[14] Wilson, G., *The Life of the Hon. Henry Cavendish* (London: Cavendish Society, 1951), p. 20.

[15] Bielschowsky, Albert, *Life of Goethe,* tr. W. A. Cooper, 3 vols. (New York: G. P. Putnam's Sons, 1905), Vol. III, p. 78.

is only then followed by the poetic idea."[16] In both art and science, then, the mechanism of Direct Analogy functions as a constructive agent of creative process.

From one of the toughest-minded successful industrial inventors of the century comes an example of Direct Analogy which occurred in the course of the invention of tetraethyl lead. "Speculating then on why kerosene knocked worse than gasoline, as it was known to do, the two men reasoned that it might be because kerosene did not vaporize as readily as gasoline. They recalled that the wild flower, the trailing arbutus, with its red-backed leaves, blooms early in spring, even under the snow. If only kerosene were dyed red, they speculated, it might—like the leaves of the trailing arbutus—absorb heat faster, and so vaporize quickly enough to burn in the engine like gasoline."[17]

The area of analogy and symbolism has been adopted by Synectics almost out of whole cloth. Mechanisms of metaphor employing Symbolic Analogy and Personal Analogy as well as Direct Analogy are implemented in our day to day experimental work. Synectics theory agrees with the conviction that a man does not know even his own science if he knows *only* it.[18]

SYMBOLIC ANALOGY

This mechanism differs from the identification aspect of Personal Analogy in that Symbolic Analogy uses objective and impersonal images to describe the problem. The individual effectively uses this analogy in terms of poetic response. He summons up an image which, though technologically inaccurate, is esthetically satisfying. It is a compressed description of the function or elements of the

[16] Schmitz, L. D., *Correspondence between Schiller & Goethe*, 2 vols., tr. L. D. Schmitz (London: George Bell & Sons, 1879), Vol. I, p. 154.

[17] Boyd, T. A., *Biography of C. F. Kettering* (New York: E. P. Dutton, 1957), p. 100.

[18] Whitehead, A. N., *The Aims of Education* (New York: Macmillan, 1929).

problem as he views it. In the course of making the problem familiar to himself, the chemist employs extensive quantitative tools. When using the mechanism of Symbolic Analogy he views the problem qualitatively with the condensed suddenness of a poetic phrase. The major difference between Symbolic Analogy and the other mechanisms is quantitative. In Personal Analogy the process of identification takes a long while for all the nuances to be expressed. A Direct Analogy may be quite straightforward but uncovering the comparison of its conceptual ramifications requires substantial time. A Symbolic Analogy is immediate. Once made, in a blurt of association, it is there, complete![19]

The cultural bifurcation of art and science in our society, and the prevalence of advanced trade schools where limited experts are ground out of the curriculum, tend to make it difficult for technical graduates to understand or use the esthetic qualitative mechanisms. However, as we have observed in the case of the other mechanisms, their use can be learned, not abstractly, but through practice. They are used apprehensively at first, but when the student sees them work, producing rich viewpoints which lead to a basic solution, even the apprehensive individual is willing to use such mechanisms to an increasing degree.

Example of Symbolic Analogy: A Synectics group was presented with this problem: How to invent a jacking mechanism to fit into a box not bigger than four by four inches yet extend out and up three feet and support four tons. The application was to be toward moving objects like houses and loads of freight. At the time, common practice was to exert initial displacement with a mechanical or hydraulic jacking mechanism which was small enough to fit into the available opening. This jack with movement limited by the ram length would push the load to the extent of its capability, then the workman replaced it with a larger and then a larger and then a

[19] Kohler, Wolfgang, *Gestalt Psychology* (London: G. Bell and Sons Ltd., 1930), pp. 207–231. Symbolic Analogy is a Gestalt response where the physical, neural, and mental patterns of activity are suddenly integrated into a compressed articulation.

larger unit. It was apparent that there was a need for one unit to do this job instead of a series.[20] In this case the group employed Symbolic Analogy to look at jacks in a new way:

A: . . . how about a biological jack where the power source would be a kind of virus culture. You drop some "food" into the culture and the animals breed and occupy more space thus offering a power source.

B: I think that such zoological entities would stop increasing after their ecology got up to a pressure of a couple of pounds per square inch.

A: Yeah. I guess you're right . . . but at least it's not another ratchet.

C: I wonder if the secret to this problem is energy or instrument?

D: It can't be energy because you could always drive it with a flexible shaft from an electric motor. You would not have to put the motor in there . . . just use the flexible shaft.

E: You could use a slow burning powder that would develop energy as you added oxygen to it.

B: But how would you fit in the actual mechanical moving element which would transfer the power?

A: This goddamn conundrum is like the Indian rope trick! Let the client go to some Indian fakir for the job.

C: It goes in soft and comes out hard . . . goes in soft and comes out hard . . .

D: What the hell are you talking about! . . . Comes out hard!

C: The Indian rope trick. The rope is soft when the guy starts with it. He shows it to everybody. The whole magic is how he makes it hard so he can climb up on it.

E: The penis does this hydraulically.

C: I like this Indian rope trick way of thinking. . . . How could we build a powerful Indian rope trick . . . strong enough to hold up many tons?

[20] Another application was a space-saving replacement for traditional bulky airplane landing gear, particularly a problem in jets.

E: No joke . . . you could do it hydraulically.

B: How?

E: It's obvious. Just collapse a rubber tube into the four inches they're allowing us . . . then pump water or oil into it under high pressure. . . .

B: It would wobble all over hell.

E: Put it inside a telescopic shaft . . . in fact the telescopic shaft could *be* the collapsible thing . . . just pump it up. . . . Oh! That would mean beautifully machined parts . . . and seals. . . . Jesus me beads, what a sealing hooligan. . . . But what's wrong with the rubber tube?

A: Somehow I'd feel safer if the damn thing were made of good steel. . . . If I have to rely on it for my life I don't want some God damn condum. . . .

B: You could reinforce the rubber . . . but this is getting crappy now . . . it hasn't got the elegance of the Indian rope trick concept. . . . We lost it somewhere.

C: How could steel go in soft and come out hard?

B: That's what a steel tape measure does. It comes out and that little bend in it stiffens it enough so that you can actually hold it out in front of you a ways . . . then it all rolls up into the case.

E: But you can't hold up anything with it . . . it would collapse.

B: Put two of them back to back so that they stiffen each other. . . . Have them separate in the case and join as they come out so that they become a monolith.

A: You know bicycle chains can only bend in one direction. They fold right up in the other direction. If you put two of them into a case and designed the thing so that when they come out of the case they were linked they would be as stiff as you needed, yet would roll up tight as hell.

E: I like that . . . I really like that but I'm bothered about how to link the two chains . . . that's tough . . . just saying it doesn't do it.

C: I bet if you just tied them together at the top that they would stay together . . . that's the way they're built.

A model was built based on the Symbolic Analogy of the Indian rope trick. It functioned exactly as described in the session.

Maxwell, for instance, made mental images to represent the elements of every problem—symbols without words. They were a kind of private painting.[21] And Sir Francis Galton said, ". . . I fail to arrive at the full conviction that a problem is fairly taken on by me, unless I have continued somehow to disembarrass it of words."[22] Both Maxwell and Galton used the mechanism of Symbolic Analogy to get away from the familiar over-rationalized, word-intoxicated view of a problem.

FANTASY ANALOGY

For Sigmund Freud, creative work in general, and art in particular, is the fulfilment of a wish, although he does not say, as he has been accused of saying, that it is nothing but a wish. The artist must know how to transform, to depersonalize, to hide the source of his wish. When he is successful in so doing, and his work is accepted, then he has accomplished through fantasy what he could have won in no other way. The wish-fulfilment theory reveals the connection between the artist's motives as a human being and his chosen method of gratifying them. Success depends upon his ability to defer consummation of the wish in fantasy and to make real the wish by embodying it in a work of art.[23]

Example of Fantasy Analogy: Synectics accepts Freud's wish-fulfilment theory of art, but turns it onto technical invention as well and uses it operationally. For instance, when faced with the problem of inventing a vapor proof closure for space suits, a part of the

[21] Campbell, L., and Garrett, M., *The Life of James Clark Maxwell* (London: Macmillan, 1882), pp. 259–260.

[22] Galton, Sir James, "Thought Without Words," *Nature,* May 1887, p. 29.

[23] Freud, Sigmund, *New Introductory Lectures on Psychoanalysis* (New York: W. W. Norton, 1933), 22nd lecture; Freud, Sigmund, *An Outline of Psychoanalysis* (New York: W. W. Norton, 1949), chap. 5.

Synectics approach was to ask the question, "How do we in our wildest fantasies desire the closure to operate?"

G: Okay. That's over. Now what we need here is a crazy way to look at this mess. A real insane viewpoint . . . a whole new room with a viewpoint!

T: Let's imagine you could will the suit closed . . . and it would do just as you wanted by wishing . . . (Fantasy Analogy mechanism)

G: "Wishing will make it so . . ."

F: Shh, Okay. Wish fulfilment. Childhood dream . . . you wish it closed, and invisible microbes, working for you, cross hands across the opening and *pull* it tight. . . .

B: A zipper is kind of a mechanical bug (Direct Analogy mechanism). But not air tight . . . or strong enough. . . .

G: How do we build a psychological model of "will-it-to-be-closed"?

R: What are you talking about?

B: He means if we could conceive of how "willing-it-to-be-closed" might happen in an actual model—then we. . . .

R: There are two days left to produce a working model—and you guys are talking about childhood dreams! Let's make a list of all the ways there are of closing things.

F: I hate lists. It goes back to my childhood and buying groceries. . . .

R: F, I can understand your oblique approach when we have time, but now, with this deadline . . . and you still talking about wish fulfilment.

G: All the crappy solutions in the world have been rationalized by deadlines.

T: Trained insects?

D: What?

B: You mean, train insects to close and open on orders? 1-2-3 Open! Hup! 1-2-3 Close!

F: Have two lines of insects, one on each side of the closure—on the order to close they all clasp hands . . . or fingers . . . or claws . . . whatever they have . . . and then closure closes tight. . . .

G: I feel like a kind of Coast Guard Insect (Personal Analogy mechanism).

D: Don't mind me. Keep talking. . . .

G: You know the story . . . worst storm of the winter—vessel on the rocks . . . can't use lifeboats . . . some impatient hero grabs the line in his teeth and swims out . . .

B: I get you. You've got an insect running up and down the closure, manipulating the little latches . . .

G: And I'm looking for a demon to do the closing for me. When I will it to be closed (Fantasy Analogy mechanism), Presto! It's closed!

B: Find the insect—he'd do the closing for you!

R: If you used a spider . . . he could spin a thread . . . and sew it up (Direct Analogy).

T: Spider makes thread . . . gives it to a flea. . . . Little holes in the closure . . . flea runs in and out of the holes closing as he goes. . . .

G: Okay. But those insects reflect a low order of power. . . . When the Army tests this thing, they'll grab each lip in a vise one inch wide and they'll pull 150 pounds on it. . . . Those idiot insects of yours will have to pull steel wires behind them in order. . . . They'd have to stitch with steel. *Steel* (Symbolic Analogy mechanism).

B: I can see one way of doing that. Take the example of that insect pulling a thread up through the holes. . . . You could do it mechanically. . . . Same insect . . . put holes in like so . . . and twist a spring like this . . . through the holes all the way up to the damn closure . . . twist, twist, twist, . . . Oh, crap! It would take hours! And twist your damn arm off!

G: Don't give up yet. Maybe there's another way of stitching with steel. . . .

B: Listen . . . I have a picture of another type of stitching. . . . That spring of yours . . . take two of them . . . let's say you had a long demon that forced its way up . . . like this. . . .

R: I see what he's driving at. . . .

B: If that skinny demon were a wire, I could poke it up to where, if it got a start, it could pull the whole thing together . . . the springs would be pulled together closing the mouth. . . . Just push it up . . . push—and it will pull the rubber lips together. . . . Imbed the springs in rubber . . . and then you've got it stitched with steel! (See figure 5.)

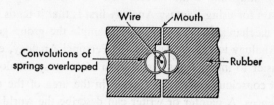

Figure 5. Cross-sectional Diagram

In the above transcription I have taken the liberty of pointing out symptoms of various mechanisms in action, but the real purpose of the transcription is to give an example of the mechanism of Fantasy Analogy. Conscious self-deceit appears in all the mechanisms to a greater or lesser degree but in the mechanism of Fantasy Analogy it is paramount. When a problem is presented to the mind it is most useful to imagine the best of all possible worlds, a helpful universe permitting the most satisfying possible viewpoint leading to the most elegant of all possible solutions.

A world where insects perform as required is this kind of universe. Common sense outlaws such fabrication which "foolishly" flies in the face of established law: How would our problem change if gravity didn't hold? What would happen to our viewpoint if entropy could be ignored? To tolerate these naive inconsistencies is irrational. It is irrational and like the other mechanisms, Fantasy Analogy has operated usually underground in the subconscious because the rational character of man denies himself and the world the vision of that part of himself which is other than proudly coherent.[24]

[24] This mechanism is akin to Freud's concept of the role of wish-fulfilment

Fantasy Analogy is particularly effective if used first in the process of making the familiar strange. This mechanism is an excellent bridge between problem-stating and problem-solving. For instance, in the preceding example, "the-willing-to-be-closed" and insect fantasy were forms of restatement of the problem in imaginative terms. The group was saying, "This closure problem is described by imagining some insects who do the closing job." Another reason for using Fantasy Analogy first is that it tends to evoke the other mechanisms. In the closure example the group goes from Fantasy Analogy to Direct Analogy to Personal Analogy, etc.

It is easier to imagine the mechanism of Fantasy Analogy operating as a conscious self-deceit fantasy in the area of the arts than in the sciences. A painter or writer can describe the world however he wishes whereas the traditional notion of the scientist is that he is limited by the phenomenological and theoretical "givens" of the world order. So long as this traditional notion is in force, technological breakthroughs will be inhibited. The technological inventor deserves and must give himself the same freedom as the artistic inventor. He must exercise the right to imagine the best (fantasy) solution to a problem while temporarily disregarding the laws defined by the implications of his solution. Only in this way can he construct an image of the ideal.

The expression "conscious self-deceit" is used to express the fact that the problem solver must be aware of the laws which conflict with his ideal solution—yet he must be willing to pretend the laws don't exist. Michael Faraday used self-deceit, as Synectics describes it, in the course of his electromagnetic research. He found that he was forced to put aside the electrical terms of his day because, "they do great injury to science, by contracting and limiting the habitual views of those engaged in pursuing it."[25] By disbelieving

---

in creative process. The difference lies in the Synectics use of self-deceit at a conscious level.

[25] Crowther, J. A., *Michael Faraday* (New York: Macmillan, 1920), p. 144.

the traditional science of his day, Faraday was able to see a more coherent hypothesis than had been realized.

The trained expert tends to be super-rational and feels threatened by any thinking which attacks his logical universe. This attitude makes breakthrough impossible. "It used to be held that God could create everything except what was contrary to the laws of logic. The truth is that we could not say of an 'unlogical' world how it would look."[26] Thus one may view a problem pretending that the laws of physics are not valid. In this way it is possible to sneak in a new way of thinking. The immutable laws usually do hold, but by pushing them out of phase for a moment one can peek in between. By the time the laws are permitted by the mind to snap back into control, the mind has derived a new viewpoint and can discover useful aberrations of the laws underlying the new viewpoint so essential for basic solution.

CONCLUSIONS

Abstractions such as intuition, deferment, empathy, play, use of irrelevance, involvement, detachment—these abstractions are almost impossible to teach because of their lack of concreteness; i.e., they are non-operational. However, the mechanisms (Direct Analogy, Personal Analogy, Symbolic Analogy, Fantasy Analogy) are psychological tools which at the conscious level almost everybody has experienced to a greater or lesser degree. Therefore it is possible to introduce them without making the individual feel that he is being manipulated. Because he correctly feels that his natural potential is being enhanced, his resistance is considerably reduced. It is absurd when dealing with rigidly conventional people to say, "let us balance a variety of irrelevancies now." On the other hand, they do not feel threatened, for instance, by an analogy from another science to

[26] Wittgenstein, Ludwig, *Tractatus Logico-Philosophicus,* (London: Routledge and Kegan Paul Ltd., 1922), p. 43.

compare with the technology implied by the problem at hand. However, the mechanism of Fantasy Analogy tends to induce the other mechanisms rather than being evoked by them.

Play with analogies covers a scale with an endless variety of levels, ranging from that which is apparent to the popular mind to that which is known only to an expert. On the simple end of the scale are analogies which are associations leading to fairly naive comparisons, such as the connection of the horse's anal sphincter with a self-sealing, self-cleaning dispenser. Applying this mechanism required no special knowledge of the physiology of the terminus of the equine lower bowel. The image of the simple sphincter function on the level of superficial perception was sufficient.

At the opposite extreme of the scale useful mechanisms derive from academic knowledge in depth. For instance, a Synectics group was attempting to solve the problem of how to invent a new kind of roof which would be more actively serviceable than traditional roofs. Analysis of the problem indicated that there might be an economic advantage in having a roof white in summer and black in winter. The white roof would reflect the sun's rays in summer so that the cost of air conditioning could be reduced. The black roof would absorb heat in winter so that the cost of heating could be minimized. The following is an excerpt from the session on this problem:

A: What in nature changes color?

B: A weasel—white in winter, brown in summer; camouflage.

C: Yes, but a weasel has to lose his white hair in summer so that the brown hair can grow in. . . . Can't be ripping off roofs twice a year.

E: Not only that. It's not voluntary and the weasel only changes color twice a year. . . . I think our roof should change color with the heat of the sun. . . . There are hot days in the spring and fall . . . and cold ones too.

B: Okay. How about a chameleon?

D: That is a better example because he can change back and forth without losing any skin or hair. He doesn't lose anything.

E: How does the chameleon do it?

A: . . . . a flounder must do it the same way.

E: Do what?

A: Hell! A flounder turns white if he lies on white sand and then he turns dark if he lands on black sand . . . mud.

D: By God, you're right: I've seen it happen! But how does he do it?

B: Chromatophores. I'm not sure whether it's voluntary or non-voluntary. . . . Wait a minute; it's a little of each.

D: How does he do it? I still don't plug in.

B: Do you want an essay?

E: Sure. Fire away, professor.

B: Well, I'll give you an essay, I think. In a flounder the color changes from dark to light and light to dark. . . . I shouldn't say "color" because although a bit of brown and yellow comes out, the flounder doesn't have any blue or red in his register. . . . Anyway, this changing is partly voluntary and partly nonvoluntary where a reflex action automatically adapts to the surrounding conditions. This is how the switching works: in the deepest layer of the cutis are black-pig-mented chromatophores. When these are pushed toward the epidermal surface the flounder is covered with black spots so that he looks black . . . like an impressionistic painting where a whole bunch of little dabs of paint give the appearance of total covering. Only when you get up close to a Seurat can you see the little atomistic dabs. When the black pigment withdraws to the bottom of the chromatophores then the flounder appears light colored . . . Do you all want to hear about the Malpighian cell layer and the guanine? Nothing would give me greater pleasure than to. . . .

C: You know. I've got a hell of an idea. Let's flip the flounder analogy over on to the roof problem. . . . Let's say we make up a roofing material that's black, except buried in the black stuff are little white plastic balls. When the sun comes out and the roof gets hot the little white balls expand according to Boyle's law. They pop through the black roofing vehicle. Now the roof is white, impressionistically white that is, à la Seurat. Just like the flounder, only with reverse English. Is it the black pigmented part of the chromatophores that come to the surface of the flounder's skin? Okay. In our roof it will be the white pigmented plastic balls that come to the surface when the roof gets hot. There are many ways to think about this . . .

The knowledge of zoology imparted by B was not childlike or naive. As contrasted to the anal sphincter analogy, the flounder analogy was backed up by technological insight without which no new viewpoint would have been possible.

Over a period of seventeen years Synectics research has observed that the richest source of Direct Analogy is biology. This is because the language of biology lacks a mystifying terminology, and the organic aspect of biology brings out analogies which breathe life into problems that are stiff and rigidly quantitative.

Although the mechanisms are simple in concept, their application requires great energy output. In fact, Synectics does not in any way make creative activity easier but rather is a technique by which people can work harder. At the end of sessions we have observed complete fatigue on the part of the participants. This fatigue comes less from the concentration involved in working through the constructive mechanism, and more from the variable balance which is so necessary. The mere stringing together of metaphors is nonproductive. Synectics participants must keep in the back of their minds the problem as understood so that they can identify those mechanisms which illuminate the problem. This oscillation between, on the one hand, apparently irrelevant analogy formation and, on the other, comparing the analogy with the elements of the problem is enormously tiring. Individuals who can learn (or who already know how) to entertain a great variety of variables without becoming confused are much more apt to be effective in a creative situation. However, the price they pay is exhaustion which is physical.

The most definitive experimental climate for testing Synectics theory has been industry. All manufacturing companies have problems for which the solutions can be valued in dollars. When Synectics groups, through the use of the Synectics mechanisms, repeatedly solve problems more efficiently than could be expected from past experience or probability alone, this implies that the mechanisms constitute at least some elements of creative process. The productivity of these groups is the research basis for continual evaluation of the general theory of Synectics. However, there are other techniques beyond the mechanisms themselves which come into play in the course of establishing experimental Synectics groups in various industries. Although Synectics has been applied successfully to such areas of problem-making, problem-solving as military defense, the theatre, public administration, and education, I take the example of the industrial model because it is the most universal, the most pragmatic, and the clearest.

The initial effort of an industrial Synectics program is directed toward product improvement or new product development. An industrial Synectics experiment should prove its value as soon as possible. The question "Is this a real improvement?" or "Do people need and want this new product?" can be answered with sufficient dispatch and certainty to judge Synectics efficiency. On the other hand the question "What should be our product policy?" or "What changes should we make in our production divisions?" does not give rise to an answer whose validity can be measured exactly or soon. For evaluating Synectics, therefore, it is in the best experimental tradition to apply the technique to product-oriented problems first.

The establishment of a Synectics Group entails three general phases:

(i) selecting personnel;

(ii) training the group;

(iii) re-integrating the group into the client environment.

Once a client has decided to establish a Synectics group in his company he is given the following eight criteria on which to base the selection of his people for interview by those persons (I will call them Synectors) responsible for the training and establishing of the group.

1. *Representation:* Men are to be selected so that their backgrounds reflect the company's operation in general: research, engineering, production, marketing, sales, finance, etc. An efficient Synectics group of five people, for instance, would consist of three technical and two non-technical members. Thus, the most obvious type of diversity is built in.[1]

Further, from talking to people—each for a period of six to ten hours—who are working in the many parts of a client company operation, interviewers get some insight into what kinds of new products the client will tolerate. Since initially Synectics theory will be applied to pragmatic product problems so that its effectiveness can be judged by the quality of its solutions, it is crucial to know enough about the company personality to make judgments later as to the practical value to the client of any given solution. Therefore, even if a candidate turns out to be unqualified for Synectics, much can be learned from discussing in depth his view of his company.

2. *Energy Level:* Candidates should have a high energy level, but management may confuse high energy level with manic behavior; Synectors are responsible for weeding out interviewees whose frantic activity gives the appearance of great output but is merely a symptom of destructive inner compulsion. A particular type of man to

[1] Whether candidates come from research and development or are drawn from all over a company depends on what role is desired for the group. Some Synectics groups limit their activity to technical problems. Other groups, such as the one described in this chapter, serve as a problem-solving tool for the company as a whole.

guard against in the final selection process is the individual who complains that he's never been given a "chance." Usually this kind of individual freezes as soon as freedom is offered him. When he no longer can blame his failure on lack of opportunity, he may exhibit great ingenuity in destroying the effectiveness of the group.

A few years ago, when the selection technique was not as positive as today, a Mr. X was chosen for Synectics group activity because of his imagination as well as apparent energy resources. Although his complaints about not having been given a chance (he'd been with the client company more than ten years) gave pause to the interviewers, the intelligent and sensitive company staff psychologist persuaded them to pick Mr. X. During the first few months of training Mr. X appeared to function most constructively. He grasped the theory as well as could be expected and contributed to the group. However, from tapes of sessions held by the group in their own quarters it was apparent that the group was singularly nonproductive. For some weeks these aimless sessions continued before it became obvious that Mr. X was ingeniously sand-bagging the effort. Dissatisfied with whatever problem they attacked, he searched for the Holy Grail, a solution that would be a panacea for all the ills of the world. His comments were too virtuous to be maligned by his co-workers, and when mildly questioned by them he evoked religious ideals for sanction. He resisted any insight into the harm he was doing or his motives. He refused to recognize the fact that his search for the perfect problem was a way of avoiding failure in solving a less perfect one. (Later the staff psychologist confessed that he had been aware of Mr. X's self-destructive tendencies but had urged Mr. X's selection because he felt that Synectics was his only hope.) If the responsibility of the Synectors had been therapeutic rather than productive they would have worked along with Mr. X. Under the circumstances he was removed, but not before he had almost undermined the group.

3. *Age Requirements:* As for any operation demanding high energy output and unconventional action, candidates should be over 25 and under 40. In the industrial situation Synectors must be

tough-minded in selecting Synectics group members. A man is no{
formed sufficiently for his Synectics potential to be judged until h{
has been on earth for 25 years. By the same token, after a man ha{
lived for forty years his personality usually takes a psychologica{
set, limiting his tolerance of new experiences. This is not to say tha{
there are *no* men under 25 or over 40 who would make excellen{
industrial Synectics participants. However, the probability of findin{
them is low and the process would incur an unnecessary expens{
from the client point of view.

Five years ago, in an attempt to achieve further diversity, an ex{
perimental group was formed using people from various age brack{
ets. However, not only was the kind of difficulty outlined abov{
encountered, but there was *too much* diversity of stature in th{
company, salary, and point of view. At present, therefore, member{
of a Synectics group are about the same age and in approximately
the same salary levels.

4. *Administrative Potential:* The ability to generalize, basic t{
Synectics, is also present in good administrators. Therefore, gen{
eralizers turn up from the client selection process which include{
the criterion of "administrative potential." Furthermore, this cri{
terion increases the probability of Synectics technique ultimately
being introduced at levels of increased management responsibility{
Personnel with administrative ability inevitably rise in a company{
If they have been trained in Synectics they will bring with them the
capacity for concrete yet imaginative problem-stating and problem-
solving in group structure. Thus administrative and policy meeting{
which had previously reflected the lowest common denominator of
the views of the participants can become Synectics sessions where
truly imaginative action results (see page 145).

5. *Entrepreneurship:* In an industrial setting the group must con{
tain the flavour of entrepreneurship. Therefore group member{
should be selected on the basis of accepting the responsibility for
success or failure independent of management's sanction. The
group should feel itself apart from its company, yet hinged to it.
If the group is too close to the company, too controlled, then its

potential will be reduced. Obviously the client wants a Synectics group to give him the economic advantages of new viewpoints. If the company engorges the group, inhibiting its entrepreneurship, it will force the group back into the mold which it was set up to transcend. The spirit of entrepreneurship introduces into a big corporation the element of vitality which is symbolic of a small hungry company. Thus the large organization gets the best of both worlds—the power of great size and the lean swiftness associated with small size.

6. *Job Background:* Ideally, people selected should have had a wide number of jobs in the company. Diversity of in-company experience will give them a broad knowledge of the company. Also, such work diversity may mean that at least unconsciously management has been grooming them for overall positions of responsibility. Although job-jumping simply may reveal dissatisfaction everywhere he was tried, a man with such a history is apt to be worth interviewing. Sometimes it is just his impatience which is intolerable to a slow-moving, conservative client; and yet this very factor may be exactly what the client needs in his Synectic group.

7. *Education:* The only operationally useful educational criterion for a given selectee is a record of having shifted fields of major interest. If he started out in biology it would be useful if he took his graduate degree in physics, thus having built into himself the knowledge to draw on for creative metaphoric comparisons. This is true of non-technical people as well. The metaphoric potential of a salesman with an academic background in one of the physical sciences exceeds that of a salesman whose studies were limited to the social sciences or literature. (By the expression "metaphoric potential" I mean the background of knowledge from which metaphors and analogies can be drawn if an individual can learn to balance parallel but separate ideas.)

8. *The "Almost" Individual:* From time to time we have met a man who has every characteristic to make him tremendously productive, but for some reason his work remains mediocre. This kind of person—if he conforms to the final selection criteria—may be

able to liberate his unplumbed potential in a Synectics environment. Therefore we like to interview such people if they can be identified. Obviously candidates of this type must be screened for personality flaws, but in our experience these flaws show up in the final selection process.

Because of the morale problem which can result from the attitude of personnel rejected after interviews by the Synectors, explaining the reason for the interview is critical. Client companies are sensitive to this potential danger and have their own ways of dealing with it. However, some suggestions are offered:

(i) The client should explain that he is experimenting with establishing a problem-solving group.

(ii) The client should imply that the prerequisites for membership in this group are less intellectual capacity and more a matter of the particular experience of the candidate. Thus the candidate can rationalize his rejection.

(iii) The client should state that selection or rejection in this group will not immediately affect the candidate's status in the company.

The selectees visit the Synectors singly and are interviewed, by those responsible for the Synectics project, over a period of eight or ten hours, starting not later than one or two p.m. and running through dinner. The purpose of so long an interview is to observe the candidate in the widest possible range of situations. The following are the criteria for this final selection:

(i) *Metaphoric Capacity:* The candidate's language is carefully watched for signs of metaphor and analogy as described by the operational mechanisms: Personal Analogy, Symbolic Analogy, Direct Analogy, and Fantasy Analogy. The candidate is encouraged to speak metaphorically.

It usually becomes abundantly clear in the first hour of conversation with the candidate whether he has this characteristic or not. The first part of the discussion is devoted to who he is, what's his job, what does he think about his future, etc. Then the dialogue begins to take a different form.[2]

SYN—Synectics interviewer

CAN—Candidate

SYN: Do you use any part of your extra-curricular activity in your lab work? (The candidate was a physicist)

CAN: That's hard to say. I don't really have any hobbies—just fixing up the house, I guess. I don't even read much any more—just technical journals. It's a full time job to keep up with what's going on in my field—optics.

SYN: I've noticed with myself that sometimes the most commonplace occurrence at home can give an insight to work at the lab.

CAN: I think I know what you mean. My kids teach me while I'm trying to teach them. We do a lot of simple experiments together—you know the type—little generators and the like.

SYN: What do you mean "they teach you"?

CAN: Well—kids look at things differently. For instance, I've got a boy nine years old, crazy about fishing. I'm not, he is, but I take him once in a while. One day we were out in the boat and he asked me what a fish saw from under the water. I tried to explain to him—you know—refractive index. Then later I looked up fish and found their eyes are different. But Bud said he still couldn't get the feeling. So he and I went swimming—each drawing a lure through the water for the other to look at from the bottom. Sure I know about refractive index, but seeing that lure from the bottom gave me a feeling. . . . I don't know how to explain it—as though I were a fish and *really* understood. . . . It was kind of fun.

---

[2] The dialogues in this section are compressed excerpts from interviews which extended over a ten hour period. During this time the critically revealing statements were widely scattered.

From the above discussion this can be learned about the candidate:

(a) Because he is sensitive to children's attitudes and treats them with playful seriousness, in a Synectics session he will listen tolerantly to and draw on the "childish" amateurishness of non-technical members.

(b) He became interested enough in fish to check on ichthyological optics, thus showing an ability to involve himself in apparent irrelevancies.

(c) His underwater exploit symbolized his experimental bent—the desire to stop mere speculation and act.

(d) In identifying himself with a fish he used Personal Analogy.

Another example of an interview follows, this time with a chemical engineer:

SYN: How did you happen to switch from English literature to chemical engineering?

CAN: It's hard to remember. I guess I thought it would be easier to get a job with a chemical engineering background.

SYN: Was it?

CAN: Well, I don't know how tough it would have been to land a position coming from English literature—but I've done all right with chemical engineering.

SYN: What interested you most in English literature?

CAN: Believe it or not—poetry.

SYN: That's a big jump—from poetry to chemical engineering.

CAN: Maybe, maybe not. . . . For instance in Paradise Lost—Milton says "Who overcomes by force, hath overcome but half his foe."

SYN: That's connected with chemistry?

CAN: Sure. Let's say you put some water and some oil in a blender and beat the mixture till you get an apparent emulsion—but it's just a temporary emulsion. In a few minutes the oil droplets no longer are caught in a continuous matrix of water—all the oil and water are completely separated on their own, i.e., force doesn't work. . . . However, if you put in a wetting agent like a household detergent and mix the oil and water the emulsion will be much more permanent.

This candidate was not embarrassed to oscillate between literature and technology and his symbolic analogy from Milton shows that he should perform well Synectically, other qualifications considered.

The following excerpt is from an interview with a man who was in production:

SYN: How in the devil did you go from biology in college to production in a company whose products are essentially electronic hardware?

CAN: I studied biology because I liked it—as a child I liked it, so when I got to the university I decided to major in it.

SYN: Do you use biology in your work?

CAN: Hardly. There's no biology in a line of amplifiers moving along a two hundred foot belt.

SYN: I still don't understand how you got into production.

CAN: When I first came to work they didn't know what to do with me. I really don't know why they hired me except it was right after the war and people were hard to get. Anyway, they put me to work in the accounting department.

SYN: For how long?

CAN: About a year. I didn't like it much and was looking for a way to get out, but I needed the money.

SYN: How did you get out?

CAN: Well, there was a foundry connected with the factory where I was, and no one wanted to work there . . . too dirty I guess. The company was looking for a young guy to work his way up in the foundry so I took it.

SYN: How was it?

CAN: After accounting it was great. But I had learned something in accounting, although I hadn't realized it—I found that I was aware of certain inefficiencies. . . . It's funny though . . . the first few months I was in the foundry I was able to pick out more troubles than after being there a year.

SYN: How long were you in the foundry?

CAN: Two years.

SYN: . . . and what were you doing about "picking out troubles"?

CAN: The first week in the foundry a couple of ways we were doing things seemed terribly slow to me so I talked to the foreman about them and the two of us figured out simpler techniques . . . but when I'd been there a while I became increasingly less critical—the process was too familiar, and right or wrong I took it for granted.

SYN: It would have been great if you could have known all about foundry work, yet somehow make it strange—wouldn't it?

CAN: I've even thought about how to do just that—but no dice. I don't know how.

SYN: I assume you liked production. Did you ever go back to accounting?

CAN: Actually I'd been more on the purchasing end of things.

SYN: Well did you ever go back to purchasing?

CAN: No! Purchasing has a funny effect on you. There you are spending large sums of money like a big shot . . . ordering huge amounts of things. After a while you think the money's yours. You get corrupted. I saw this happen to some of the men. They actually lived in a phantasy world at the office. They must have had a hell of a shock every night when they got home.

SYN: But you did like production.

CAN: I still do. I like playing God. I push the button and the line moves. Elements come onto the main belt and are assembled and at the end is the finished product. The whole thing is a mechanical birth process.

This candidate showed an innate grasp of the problem of making the familiar strange and the mechanism of Direct Analogy. Also his insightful account of the purchasing staff's self deception showed that his mind was metaphorical in general.

The following interview was with a salesman:

SYN: What did you do in college when you weren't studying anthropology?

CAN: That's why I was in anthropology—I didn't have to study—plenty of time for carousing.

SYN: I'm afraid that was my feeling in college too. It wasn't till I went back as a veteran after the war that I learned anything.

CAN: I really enjoyed anthropology—in fact I thought seriously about going to graduate school. But I got married my last year in college and had to go to work. My wife was pregnant. I was too young to know how to have avoided it.

SYN: Do you use anthropology in your work?

CAN: My God no! But if you could see some of my customers you'd think I was collecting anthropological specimens.

SYN: Do you like selling?

CAN: I love it—it's like a show to me,—drama that is.

SYN: How come?

CAN: Well, I make out in my mind a whole script before I visit a customer. I spend quite a bit of time on it but when you're selling construction equipment each sale represents thousands of dollars so I figure it's worth the time.

SYN: How much time does it take?

CAN: That's hard to say—sometimes I make two or three alternative scripts—and I use whichever one fits either my mood or the mood I find the customer in.

SYN: Can you remember any scripts?

CAN: Sure. My largest customer is a man with terrible ulcers. I noticed that he was always worse in the morning so I never called on him till the middle of the afternoon. I knew he needed about $200,000 of earth moving equipment and I was hot to sell him.

Syn: How did you know?

Can: He told me. He said he hadn't decided whether to place the order with us or our competitor.

Syn: What kind of script did you write?

Can: Well, first I cast my play. I made my customer into a father of a beautiful girl and I was one of two suitors. The daughter was the $200,000 order.

Syn: My God—where did you go from there?

Can: Well, in the script the suitor tries to tell the girl's father why he'd make a good husband for his daughter. He tells him how much he earns, how good his family is, and so on. But the father keeps saying he's no different, better or worse, than the competitive suitor. Finally, in desperation, the suitor says he loves the girl more and therefore he'll treat her better.

Syn: How did you use this one act job?

Can: The girl was the order, you remember. The suitor was I. The father was my customer and the other suitor was the competitor. Actually our competitor's stuff *is* just as good as ours so I interpreted my script in terms of telling the customer I wanted the order more than the competitor and I would take better care of it—service, delivery, etc.

Syn: But did you get it?

Can: Darn right!

Syn: But wasn't your ultimate sales pitch rather traditional? About "wanting the order more," I mean?

Can: It's difficult for me to explain the difference. I've been selling heavy construction equipment for 8 years and of course I've used the gimmick before . . . the gimmick of "wanting" a customer's order. But when I was playing out the script, my attitude, how I felt, was different. . . . The $200,000 order and the beautiful daughter became mixed in my mind. My attitude wasn't commercial. I *wasn't* just after the dough. I was in love with the order, I wasn't too articulate. . . . I was terribly honest and earnest . . . not smooth and slick.

This man developed a wonderful Fantasy Analogy. Then he made a Direct Analogy from it. He was freely able to identify with the imaginary suitor through Personal Analogy. Unfortunately, in interviews the operational mechanisms are not always so apparent; but when they are specially listened for, and are present, they can be identified by trained Synectors.

(ii) *Attitude of Assistance:* Because some characteristics of a candidate can't be identified from conversation alone, the interview includes taking a walk in the woods, inviting the candidate to participate in a project on the property (pipe is being laid or a little bridge is being built over a stream, or a new timber is being fitted to the barn); in the evening the candidate meets with the Synectors for a cook-out. If his attitude of assistance has not revealed itself before, the cook-out preparation is used as the ultimate test. In general there are three kinds of response to this activity:

   (a) The candidate sits and watches the fire being laid.
   (b) The candidate asks if he can help.
   (c) The candidate observes what is needed and supplies it.

Building a fire is such a universal function, known to everyone, that it serves as an excellent test of assistance attitude. Obviously, for the purpose of Synectics, a man who sees how he can help and does it is the most acceptable. Part of the fire making technique is to make sure that there is not enough kindling on the spot so as to guarantee ample opportunity for the candidate to reveal himself.

(iii) *Kinesthetic Coordination:* Although clumsiness is not inconsistent with creative potential, Synectors guard against selecting a man whose extreme lack of coordination implies a lack of self-confidence. As described in (ii), the interview involves many opportunities for varieties of physical exertion. Allowing for the candidate's self-consciousness due to the interview situation, it is still remarkably revealing to observe his handling, for instance, of the end of a twenty foot timber. Does he use his body efficiently, or does he depend on brute strength? Does he grasp the timber in a comfortable spot or just clutch it anywhere? Has he planned where he will put his feet when he moves to put the timber in position? If a candidate exhibits good coordination then he has passed this criterion. If he is clumsy, there may be extenuating circumstances. Is he afraid someone will let his end fall, thus endangering him? Is fear of this accident making him appear more inept than usual? Should there be no explanation and should the candidate perform poorly in three or four situations, it is assumed that some internal conflict attends him and unless he scores very highly in each of the other criteria he is turned down. However, no candidate has ever passed all the rest of the criteria, then failed the kinesthetic one.

(iv) *Risk:* In the course of talking to the candidate, Synectors must determine whether he enjoys taking risks and, if so, what kind of risks. Is the candidate a self-destructive gambler who is unconsciously trying to injure himself? Is he willing to risk because he knows it's the only way to accomplish certain tasks? Does he enjoy risking or does it frighten him? The candidate's attitude toward risk appears in many ways, for instance:

SYN: We're sorry your wife could not come along with you.

CAN: Me too—but she's seven months pregnant and the doctor didn't want to have her travel. . . . Anyway she claims she's had enough traveling this year to last her a while.

SYN: Have you moved recently—changed jobs?

CAN: No, not that. Last summer, instead of building an addition to the house we blew the money on a trip to Europe—kids and all. Neither my wife nor I had ever been abroad and . . . we could make the addition later, but someone might set fire to Paris.

SYN: How did the children like it?

CAN: They were a bit too young, I guess—5 and 8—but they got a kick out of it . . . when I got off the plane at LaGuardia I had 15¢ in my pocket. But it was worth it.

The above dialogue shows a candidate whose sense of value called for spending all his money on a trip—this meant more to him than adding to his house. He even said later that he considered the house addition to be a status symbol rather than something his family really needed. This candidate's impetuous voyage actually was an investment in an important experience—a most constructive risk from the Synectics point of view.

(v) *Emotional Maturity:* Creative people tend to have a child-like quality about them, but this childishness is not neces-sarily a sign of emotional immaturity. The emotionally im-mature childlike person does not use his childlike surprise, wonder, and infinite curiosity about the world as a psycho-logical basis for creative acts (see Chapter II, page 129). It is the capacity to integrate childishness into constructive acts which the Synectors look for in their interviews with candidates. Candidates' conversation is watched carefully for this quality, but as with many of the criteria, this one is best observed in vivo. For example, while walking through the woods does the candidate show interest in the habits of animals, in the plant life, in the rock formation of the stream bed? By interest I do not mean mere intellectual speculation. Does he experiment? Does he trace an animal track? Does he take a leaf in his fingers and feel its quality? Does he find a place in the stream where he can observe the stratum? In the course of participating in a project such as building a small dam, can the candidate throw himself into the job with childlike abandon? Is the preparation of the supper fire a chore or fun for him? Conversation alone may reveal the candidate's interest in many things . . . he may read broadly. This trait is significant but perhaps he never puts to use the knowledge gained. When he is encouraged to participate as described, a judgment of him can be relied on.

(vi) *The Capacity to Generalize:* What are the candidate's thinking habits? Can he take three or four facts and construct from them a straightforward, conversational, coherent generalization? Can he oscillate from particular facts to theories which embrace and integrate the facts? A generalization is a hypothesis describing and including diverse and sometimes conflicting data. Can the candidate defer from generalizing on the basis of facts too few and too soon? Can he tolerate the ambiguity with which he must live until a soothing, all-ordering generalization explains the data? And then can he act on the basis of his generalization? The first form of action is to compare his generalization with more facts of the same family as the facts made coherent by his generalization. The second activity phase is to build a model, physical or conceptual, to test his generalization. Is he afraid of testing his generalization for fear it will not survive the hard test of reality? The candidate's generalizing level can be judged positively from talking to him. His normal habits of action relative to generalization can be deduced intuitively. However, if he is a good generalizer there is a high probability that the other members will complement him even if his action response is meager.

(vii) *Commitment:* If the candidate believes in something—product or a concept—can he commit himself to bringing it to life? Or is he self-protectively analytical and falsely sophisticated? The personality characteristic of enthusiasm is not by itself a guarantee. The candidate must identify with a project so that its success is crucial to him. Since not all projects "win" he must be able to fight off the bitterness which might result from losing. The Synectors weigh the data of the interview and make a guess on this criterion—a judgment based on past experience. Doubtful candidates can be carefully observed during the early stages of their training.

(viii) *Non-status Oriented:* There are traditional symbols of status in American industrial society: carpet on the floor, large clean desks, prints on the wall, name on the door, in charge of a large number of men, conservatively natty clothes, new car—these symbolize the position of a man. Minor variations are permitted within the conventions of this framework to describe the residual differences in personalities. People chosen for Synectics activity must be beyond status as defined by the traditional symbolism because their group will develop another kind of status based on contribution and independence. Their quarters will not be orderly and antiseptic but should reflect the energy and enthusiasm of the group. They come to work dressed as they please, prepared for the laboratory or the machine shop. They will be judged by what they produce, not how they appear.

This criterion is easily determined. In talking to a man for six to ten hours his status-consciousness reveals itself because a status-oriented individual is proud of the symbols which have so much prestige for him.

(ix) *Complementary Aspect:* No candidate can get a perfect score in all the criteria but the group as a whole should make up 100% of the characteristics implied by the list of criteria. Also, there are certain special personality traits within the candidates which must be balanced. Assume two men who score high, one from research, one from sales. The researcher, introverted and studious, rates the salesman as flamboyant and loud. The salesman calls the researcher mousey and secretive. Each man distrusts the other, yet both are necessary to the success of a Synectics operation. Someone must be found who can bring together the researcher and salesman. The Synectors, on the lookout, decide on a man who had been in research but now, for instance, is in sales engineering. This "integrator" is interviewed, not only on the basis of the criteria, but also to learn whether his personality can resolve the conflict between the researcher and the salesman.[3] These three men then constitute an organic entity whose personality must be considered before a fourth is added. The four persons constitute another type of organic entity, and the final candidate is chosen with the purpose of ending up with a "perfectly" inter-complementary group. Later these people will be taught to understand and communicate with each other, but the Synectors must have selected a group for whom this is possible.

The training time consists of one week a month for twelve months. Before the first session, client management submits a list of five to ten problems—technical and non-technical—considered old chestnuts, which have been plaguing the client for a long while. Valuable solutions to the problems on the list constitute the best experimental evidence that the Synectics operation is in fact more effective, more productive, than any problem-solving effort in the past experience of the client. If we made up our own problems and then went ahead to solve them, it could be said that we had collected problems for which we already had the answers. There would be no certain way for the client or ourselves to judge the efficiency of the Synectics method. (Another way of judging the success of Synectics is for the client's patent department to estimate the value and degree of novelty of the concepts produced by the Synectics group as compared with the company's traditional creative efforts. This kind of checking permits the client to make judgments about the value of Synectics from time to time in the course of the program.)

[3] The "integrator" selection is the most critical of all since on him rests the responsibility of balancing the major conflicting constructive potentials in the operating group.

Starting with the first week-long session the five selectees are boarded in a separate house, which is set aside for their use. The purpose is to throw these people together so as to build *esprit* not unlike the feeling of a high-morale rifle company; and Synectics uses techniques developed for integrating small groups in World War II. Living together through Synectics training is a shared experience out of which come the private jokes and shorthand communication so indicative of a closely knit group. Complete grasp of the operational mechanisms will not by itself guarantee success in a Synectics project; therefore training of a group must go beyond imparting intellectual insight and must embrace the emotional component.

Some individuals take the immediate attitude that suggested reading is an implied attack on their whole intellectual history. Because selectees are wary of anything that smacks of "molding" them, they must understand and believe that their reading program is designed to assist them in behaving in an individualistic way. At the very beginning of training, group members are given certain books. Their reading serves three purposes:

(i) Reading increases metaphoric potential and in the reading habits of 90% of the people interviewed Synectors have observed a shocking paucity. The literature which is their cultural well is limited to technical journals, newspapers, and national weekly magazines. The group's reading program starts with literature that contains examples of the Synectics operational mechanisms in action, i.e., autobiographical accounts of innovation in art and science. The next reading phase is devoted to the life sciences—zoology, biology, physiology—because from these areas come the most effective metaphors. Reading in Synectics theory comes late in the training program because it is more effective to have selectees experience the operational mechanisms before speculating about them.

(ii) Whenever possible group members read the same book. This is a way of beginning to give diverse individuals a language in common though initially strange to all of them. In fact, a language of this sort will become common to the group to the degree that at first it is mutually strange.

(iii) The group is given books of trauma, i.e., descriptions of agony and death during polar expeditions in particular, and exploration in general as well as disasters at sea. These serve two functions:

    (a) group members vicariously share the same traumatic experiences. This tends to increase the bond among them;

    (b) many basic inventions satisfy basic needs and nowhere are basic needs so primitively revealed as when man is faced with elemental privation.

The first weekly session indoctrinates the selectees into the actual use of the mechanisms of Synectics and into group commitment to solve the problems presented to them by their management. The group is encouraged to see the life of their company as depending on their efforts, and during this period members are persuaded to examine the morality of their employer. They ask themselves questions. In the condition of the world today does it make any sense to worry about the survival of any element of industry? If not, why be excited about the future of their company? If so, what is so worthy about their company? Is their employer more than just a source of income for them? If not, how can the company be improved?

Energy to implement a Synectics project in our culture must be grounded in conviction about morality and social value. Research during the war was enormously productive because, among other things, it was motivated by the excitement of "fighting on the right side" for survival. Synectics theory attempts to establish within a group a tone of attenuated crisis. The group recognizes where its industry fits into the American economy and how this economy may survive only if it is fed basically new products. The United States is competing with the rest of the world and the nation's success may depend on a small way on the creative capacity of this group.

Another morale-building feature is the thrill of arriving—of participation in constructing a solution. In the early days of a group, members listen over and over to a tape where they made a conceptual breakthrough. Part of the training technique entails auditing tapes, since in this way selectees can best understand the use of the mechanisms. The fact that all sessions are being tape recorded is never hidden from the group in training. Although some self-consciousness exists at first, this is overcome by the early realization that the tape recording is a confidential teaching tool, an evocative memory device, and a source of excitement for reliving a breakthrough. The group listens to a "breakthrough" tape to re-experience the thrill, the feeling of sudden glory, which is highly sexual in its climatic aspect. Thus, as soon as possible the group becomes motivated by a variety of factors:

(a) the in-group feeling derived from shared experience;

(b) the morality of their action;

(c) crisis;

(d) creative responsibility;

(e) excitement in "winning."

Observations of housekeeping reveal the particular selectee who has the greatest amount of leadership prestige for the rest of the group (housekeeping tools and food are supplied but not servants). As homely jobs arise, such as cooking breakfast and making beds, one person soon persuades the others to make decisions about responsibility for various chores, not authoritatively but off-handedly. When the group is finally integrated back into the client company it will have to have an administrative head, and it is important to identify this person as early as possible. The ideal leader combines initiative in routine chores with leadership in sessions.

Session leadership depends on four main characteristics:

(i) Extreme Optimism: The leader should believe that anything is possible—not idiotically, but from enthusiasm about the eternal presence of possibility;

(ii) Total Grasp: The leader should have had the widest experience in life and in industry so that he can best integrate and interpret all possible concepts and associations;

(iii) Synectics Grasp: The leader must have understanding in depth of Synectics in general;

(iv) Psychical Distance: More than other members of the group the leader must keep himself sufficiently distanced from the session process to steer it constructively. He must never become so involved as to lose distance. He is responsible for balancing the one and the many.

In all training sessions at least two Synectors are present. When the use of mechanisms must be explained, two Synectors can act it out—one Synector would have to describe it abstractly. Also, two Synectors can transcend the authoritarianism associated with teaching by naturally, and without pressure, giving examples of how Synectics functions.

Since the selectees have, at the outset, only a general understanding of Synectics, the first session is critical. The group is invited to initiate a direct attack on one of the given problems. The Synectors suggest a mechanism here and there, not forcibly. After working for an hour the tape is replayed and at this time the Synectors point out where the mechanisms were used properly or where they should have been used. Then the session continues for another hour, etc. This process continues until a concept or viewpoint is developed, at which time sessions are temporarily stopped. The viewpoint is tested in a preliminary, experimental fashion. The group oscillates between conceptual sessions and practical implementation. While the technical feasibility of an idea is being examined or parts are en route, the group gathers for sessions on other problems. When the parts arrive sessions cease and all group members participate in the laboratory exercise of reducing the concept to practice, checking its market prospects, or evaluating it financially.

Throughout the twelve month training period Synectors take every opportunity to have each member develop an understanding of the specialties of the other members. For instance, the salesman will help in the lab work, the chemist will make a market survey, the financial man will examine production possibilities, the physicist will make a financial analysis, the production man will outline a sales program. Thus, not only is the group brought together more closely, but standard industrial practices are looked at in a new way by someone to whom they are strange.

At the earliest opportunity the group is made to realize that it can and must move more quickly than is traditional in a large corporation. Synectors encounter inertia about testing a viewpoint at a high rate of speed. Group members coming from the sophisticated climate of a large corporation are too "philosophical," too patient with bottlenecks such as procurement lag. However, when mechanical and psychological techniques for jumping these hurdles are grasped by the group, the members become quick to take action. For instance, one group needed some special products which could be produced only in a wood finish mill. The estimated time of delivery was six weeks. The group members were disappointed but passively willing to accept the six week delay as a necessary part of life. To give them the actual experience of speeding implementation they were bundled into the car and driven down to see the foreman at the finish mill. The foreman was stirred to excitement about the project and brought into the invention as a participant; he and his men worked enthusiastically until late that night to have the parts ready early the next morning.

From the first day, Synectors are on guard for symptoms of guilt on the part of group members. Even though the group members are working sixteen hours a day, the experience is so new and they enjoy themselves so much that it is impossible for them to disregard the ethic which holds that work must be onerous. When such a feeling of guilt appears, the only certain way to transcend it is for the group to have a conceptual and practical success. The success sanctions the attendant pleasure, and guilt is replaced with constructive excitement. Once a group has worked through the experience of guilt transcended, it is made to understand what has happened to it. Ultimately the group must understand the process of its own education so the members can act as the didactic heart of Synectics activity when they are reintegrated into their parent company.

When selectees arrive for the first weekly sessions they inevitably have preconceived notions of what will happen to them. A recurrent anxiety is that they will be pressed into a mold to conform with the precepts of Synectics. They imagine that Synectics implies certain personality characteristics to which they must adhere. Told this is not true, they interpret this denial as an attempt to throw them off guard for the purpose of more effective Synectics brainwashing. The Synectors in charge of the teaching program must prove sincerity in other ways. For example, in early sessions selectees actually try to conform to a mold the shape of which they do not know and the existence of which has been protested. Each selectee must be encouraged to contribute according to the operational mechanisms, of course, but in terms of his special personality traits. When a selectee continually articulates his thoughts along over-rational lines the session is halted immediately. He is told the reasons for expressing himself personally, unedited, rather than making statements which are cold and analytical. He must be made to believe that he is accepted as a person, not just for sentimental reasons of human justice but because the quality of his Synectics contributions are founded in his particular sensitivities and responses.

Another recurrent attitude manifest during the early days of a Synectics program is cynicism. Why do the selectees accept the job if they query the validity of Synectics theory? Because they do not want to reveal lack of ambitious interest to their management. Because they are not *certain* that Synectics theory is ineffectual. Because they are flattered at being chosen. Because they *do* want to take advantage of Synectics if it does work. This cynicism, not necessarily unhealthy, continues till a definite success is realized. If a success comes too soon two results follow:

(i) The group may change from an attitude of doubt to a position of fanatical religious acceptance, blind and childlike. Group members are aware that the problem they are attacking has been unsuccessfully assailed for years at great expense; and "winning" reduces their critical faculties;

(ii) The group members, having "won" once and so easily, think they are ready to take off on their own. When this overconfidence arises there is no point in arguing against it. Instead, arrangements are made for the group members to have sessions by themselves. Encountering defeat over a period of days, they are forced to re-examine their confidence and take up their student roles again.

Actually whenever the group feels ready to try Synectics on its own it is wise to encourage this independence. Otherwise it may become so dependent on the Synectics professionals that it never can break away on its own. Therefore, from time to time in the course of the program the group is encouraged to experiment with autonomous sessions. Tapes are made of these and reviewed by the Synectors. Then the taped sessions are criticized by Synectors and group members so that errors in technique are revealed. There is no question about when a particular group is prepared to become integrated back into the parent client company. Group members are ready, after they have held repeated successful sessions by themselves, to go into the final phase of the program.

The job of establishing a Synectics group for a client takes about a year. Initial selection by the client management and Synectors' final decision is completed by the end of the first month. The second, third and fourth months are occupied with training; the selectees spend one week a month training with the Synectors and the other three weeks at their regular jobs. At the end of the fourth month the prospective Synectics group presents to its management solutions to the problems chosen for it to work on. At the time of this presentation, management can make its first measure of the effectiveness of Synectics theory in terms of days and dollars spent. The results of this first third of the program are only concepts, viewpoints and the most preliminary of feasibility studies; but even at this early date management may sense the excitement and enthusiasm of the group. More important, however, the viewpoints will be new and promising. The fourth, fifth and sixth months are devoted to teaching and problem-solving on the same time schedule. At the end of the sixth month some implementation of new concepts is completed and the group again reports to management. (Synectors do not attend any of these presentations.) At this time, not only concepts are described but also preliminary research relative to market potential and technical feasibility. Again, management has an opportunity to judge the efficiency of the Synectics operation, not only intuitively as from the first report, but by the actual models shown. At this time management also should inquire of its patent experts as to the rate and inventive quality of this group's production relative to other efforts of which the patent department may be aware.

During the last six months of the Synectics teaching program the group in training continues to devote one week a month to this activity. The last half of the program consists of:

(i) Continued teaching of Synectics theory of solution techniques with special emphasis on how to train others;

(ii) Determining what the organizational posture of the Synectics group should be in the parent company.

Starting with the seventh month the Synectics group will continue actual problem-solving sessions primarily on its own. Synectors gradually absent themselves from actual sessions, but keep in touch by auditing tapes. If the Synectors notice trouble they rejoin the group until the emergency is over, then they return to their auditing role.

Experts in various technical fields, from inside the company and outside, participate when needed. The use of experts as described before becomes a more important part of the training in this last phase of the project. Tapes are made of the group in sessions with experts. These tapes also are reviewed and criticized.

Operating within its own company, the Synectics group begins to cast about to find other people who might augment their effort. At first the group experiments tentatively with selection. Members are on the look out for people using the mechanisms naturally. In fact the client Synectics group works through all the processes by which they themselves were chosen and trained. They practice, but in practicing they identify other personnel who appear to be Synectically inclined. Ultimately the group will act as a core, a center of a continually enlarging Synectics effort, and group members must prepare themselves to act as Synectors for their company. Otherwise Synectics activity will require continuous assistance from outside and it will never become a natural part of the client's operation.

(i) The more people in a company who can function along Synectics lines, the easier it will be for the core group to draw on them for their special talents.

(ii) Certain members of the core group will advance within the administration of a company on their way to management responsibility. Other members will prefer to remain with the group but the voids in the group must be filled as they occur. By having a ring of irregulars, people who have worked with the core group on a part-time basis, it is a simple task to choose the right individuals to take the place of the departed ones.

(iii) Sometimes the best way for a Synectics operation to grow is by nucleation. One or two members of the core group spin off from it and start a satellite group, filling out their number from the irregulars.

(iv) Synectics technique is based heavily on metaphoric richness. Sooner or later any given Synectics group will notice that its effectiveness as a problem-solving tool is dropping. Their metaphors are growing stale. At this time it is essential to draw on new people to enrich the metaphor inventory. If group members have been testing possible candidates all along, they will know who can contribute a new stimulus.

During the later phase of the Synectics program when the members of the in-training group are practicing selection, they make many mistakes in choice. Recognizing that error in selection is inevitable, the group employs a revokable system for final testing. Using the ten criteria discussed in this section the in-training client group identifies what it believes to be employees with Synectics potential. One by one these are invited to spend a day or two with the core group, but they are not "on trial." They are invited to help on a specific problem, and there is no overtone of being interviewed or observed. In the course of their visit with the core group the candidates participate in sessions as well as implementation so that the core group has every opportunity to judge their Synectic capacity. If a candidate is unsatisfactory, since he "wasn't being considered for Synectics" anyway, there is no psychological problem in returning him to his regular job after his visit. Synectors assist in this selection activity by auditing tapes of sessions where a candidate was present. Then, with members of the in-training group, the candidate's contributions are criticized and his Synectics capacity is evaluated. Nothing in the whole training program is so vigorously effective as this phase. Any deficiencies in the grasp of Synectics technique reveal themselves when the core group begins to operate autonomously, but deficiencies never become so apparent as during selection practice.

It is dangerous to judge abstractly how the group should function back in the parent company when it starts out on its own. Questions of mechanics such as the location of their quarters, how to select and train others in Synectics and to whom they should report are examined during the last six-month phase. The three weeks per month spent at the home company offer the Synectics group the opportunity to experiment with various approaches to the form their activity will take, so the final decision will be based on actual experience.

During the final six-month phase considerable Synector effort is devoted to outlining, on the basis of its experiments relative to mechanics, what the group's future position should be.

When the training program is completed (after 12 months) their quarters at the home office should be separate because their modes of action are different from standard methods and the parent company will not want to risk exposing its whole organization until the value of Synectics as a total company-wide tool can be estimated. The habits of the Synectics group may conflict with traditional practices. Often group members will be doing jobs usually reserved for a laboring man and they must be free to dress accordingly. It might be an embarrassment to them or to others to have them appear in something less than the style expected of rising young executives. Their hours will tend to be bizarre. In their enthusiasm to get something finished they may work all night. Next day they may come in at noon. If their quarters are located too near a parent company facility the nine-to-five employees will be disturbed by these irregularities.

No matter how carefully the integration of the group is planned it may be regarded with jealousy, as an elite, as extra privileged. People will murmur, "If they gave me the same opportunity as those men I could really produce too." The most effective antidote to envy is for the Synectics quarters to be completely naked of company status symbols. The Synectics group should have its own shop and lab facilities. Let their tools and laboratory apparatus be secondhand, but serviceable. Let the desks be discarded wooden ones. Let the conference room be comfortable but a little "out-at-the-elbows." Let the group build a few of the bookcases or whatever else is needed. Building their own things serves the further purpose of making the group feel that their lab is a "home" where they like to be, their own. Typewriter and recording equipment should be of first quality, but files, chairs, benches and the like should not give the appearance of a Hollywood set of a research laboratory. The informal aspect of their quarters has more than one advantage:

(i) It reduces out-group envy and resistance.

(ii) It keeps the cost of the Synectics experiment to a minimum.

(iii) It reinforces the tenet that this group will be judged by its production not its pretension.

(iv) It sets the stage for unconventional thinking and action. In expensive surroundings the conversation tends to be expensive and superrational; shiny new tools are inconsistent with the imperfect, tentative process of invention.

A kitchen should be fitted into the Synectics quarters because the group will be working at times when it is impossible to find eating places open. Also the act of cooking simple dishes draws the group together and creates an atmosphere of unity and lack of conformity, a feeling of "Here, in this place, I can think and act the way I feel." As with the rest of the quarters, this kitchen should be serviceable, but not elaborate. There are other important reasons for providing the Synectics group with private quarters and laboratory facilities:

(i) The group must be free to be wrong without fear of sneers. In a research and development model shop people work from drawings—drawings which have to be worked over from an engineering point of view. The early stage of testing a concept for technical feasibility is too soon for drawings. Often models can be built without even sketches. Such efficiency can be implemented only if the group has its own facilities.

(ii) The research and development model shop, being part of a large organization, must be watched and guarded. This means that it is not always accessible. Even if it is accessible, many times the very tool needed is in use.

(iii) One of the research techniques which results from Synectics training is the art of making a model to test a principle in the quickest possible way. This early model will not give all the answers, but it will tell the group whether or not it is on the right track. To reinforce a previously made point, these early models look queer and unprofessional and the group would be embarrassed to show them. But they must be free to build them.

(iv) Invention is akin to painting for in practice, the element being constructed has the capacity to tell the builder what the next step should be. In invention this is much more critical than in engineering because the inventor is always attempting to do something new (See Autonomy of Object, page 138).

Separate quarters do not *necessarily* mean that the in-company Synectics group sets up shop miles away from any parent company installation. With secluded entry and exit means, the group may be situated in a corner of research and development. However, if there are substantial academic institutions in the environs it may be best for the group to establish residence nearby. Being near a university the group can become a little social-intellectual center. From their kitchen they can serve simple lunches or suppers. Synectics activity has appeal for academic people and they, in turn, may make valuable contributions to the group. For example:

(i) The Synectics group is educated in diverse branches of science, culture, and business. The academicians have a place to gather where they can learn about Synectics theory.

(ii) The group has the conceptual and mechanical capacity to make an idea practical. Teachers are often doing research which has commercial implications and enjoy seeing something practical come out of their inventions.

(iii) The academicians offer a wealth of metaphor, particularly the teachers of the life sciences. Professors of biology and zoology rarely capture the consulting fees of their faculty brothers in the physical sciences; therefore they welcome the opportunity to work with the Synectics group.

Thus a new leverage can be added to the overall client company research and development effort.

Much as management may want to clasp the Synectics group close to its breast, it must be persuaded to permit autonomy or else risk driving out of the group the very spirit it wants to keep alive. One of the advantages of a Synectics operation is to give a large corporation the flexibility and speed of action of a small company without losing the wealth and power of a great one. The Synectics group may be given the freedom to produce and test-market a product it has invented. Often it costs so much for a complex industrial giant to test a new product that the risk is too great. However, a small unit like a Synectics group can, with a minimum of expense, launch a new product on a limited basis—limited but sufficient to test its market acceptance. It is difficult to persuade a large company to commit itself to a program of producing and marketing a new item. I have heard a President of a large corporation say, only partly in jest, that he abhorred a promising new product idea because that meant he would have to tie up a lot of capital, time and effort to produce it. However, a large corporation must protect itself against its own built-in resistance by giving the Synectics group all possible freedom.

At the earliest possible time the new Synectics group begins to have other people from the parent company flowing through its operation. For instance, somebody who has a problem can come and live with the group for a matter of weeks. He may get his problem solved; more important, he will begin to understand Synectics theory and how it can be applied. Thus the group enlarges its potential by training others, and the company reaps the benefit. Each member of the group should spend one day a month back in the department he came from. There he will find problems lying around which are considered insoluble. He can bring these back to his group and work on them. Also, this enables the Synectics group to keep in touch with the company, while remaining independent and constructively objective. Synectics relationships with the parent company can take many physical and social forms, the exact details of which are different for each situation. However, the general pattern is constant: independent proximity.

A further training responsibility during this six months' period is presentation:

Management Presentation: Management is commonly presented with a *fait accompli* and the process by which a new product or new concept was born is never demonstrated. Management is not encouraged to participate or build on the concept that is presented. Synectics training teaches the group to present its ideas in terms of the process by which these ideas were born. In this way management can begin to feel a part of this process, can feel that it is contributing, not just coldly analyzing; and the high contributory potential among management personnel can be utilized.

Transfer Presentation: Periodically, in the course of its activity, a Synectics group must transfer a concept, or an early reduction to practice, to people who are in the best position in the company to take this concept or model further. As in management presentation, the product is described not only in terms of its present state but also in terms of the history of how it was conceived. In transfer presentation it is important for the originator to take increasingly less credit for the concept and to make the person to whom it is being transferred feel that it was his. It is difficult for a single individual to push himself out of the picture when he has invented something. He wants to be certain that he will get the credit. He wants to be congratulated. However, in the case of a group, the members can congratulate themselves while permitting somebody else to take pride in a new product or a new concept.

How are patents handled? Who gets the credit? How many names appear on an application? Patents resulting from the efforts of a Synectic group are processed traditionally. Invention records, made out following the conception of an idea in a session, are signed by all members of the group present at the session. Invention records subsequent to conception and following some preliminary reduction to practice are signed by those responsible for this investigation implementation. The final formal application is signed by those who proved the validity of the concept through experimentation and model building.

The budget for a Synectics operation is worked out on the basis of each man's salary multiplied by the company's overhead figure according to usual practice. If a company's auditing system multiplies a $10,000-a-year man's salary by three to estimate how much it costs to have him around, the budget for this man in a Synectics operation would be $30,000.00. A group of five would have an annual budget of $150,000 which is turned over to the Synectics operation to use as they see fit. Let the members fail or succeed on the basis of this budget. They buy their own tools. If they use inside consulting help let them pay for the use of these people. Obviously if they use outside experts they will have to pay. Thus the group develops the sense of autonomy and responsibility. With a budget based on standard company practices the company comptroller can more readily accept this rather radical operation as something he can account for.

The Synectics group divides its work into:

(i) Problems internally discovered;

(ii) Problems coming from other parts of the company.

The group must not trust in the parent company's patience, no matter how intense its enthusiasm at the beginning of a Synectics operation. If management sees nothing tangible within a year or so, disenchantment appears. Therefore, it is important for a Synectics group to put out a few fires each year, thus sanctioning its existence and guaranteeing its freedom to attack more fundamental problems.

Remuneration is straightforward for those group members who grow up and out of full time Synectics activity into management positions, because with management responsibility comes increased financial reward. How to reward productive group members without administrative ability is a sticky personnel problem because they must not feel discriminated against if their greatest contributions are made from within Synectics activity. One method of treating this situation is through bonuses based on specific performance rather than an over-all company performance. Every company will have its own policy on this matter, but we have observed the most satis-factory arrangement to be a Synectics operation considered as an independent entity.

THE COMMONPLACE

The commonplace is the world of naive perception, free from sophisticated semantic rationalization. The specialized semantics of established knowledge constitutes conventions which make reality abstract and second-hand. "The second-handedness of the learned world is the secret of its mediocrity."[1] Learned conventions can be windowless fortresses which exclude viewing the world in new ways.

What is frequently mistaken for the sophisticated point of view condemns the commonplace as obvious and banal and worships the purity of the superrational conventions of knowing. The pseudo-artist regards the commonplace as the abode of the Philistine; the proponent of technical *expertise* regards the commonplace as the abode of the naive. Each identifies himself with the conventions of his science or his art. Elaborate conventions tend to become works of art in themselves, but they are another's work of art which have so much prestige for the "sophisticate" that he is unwilling to fracture them in the interest of extending or transforming them. This unwillingness is as much a matter of emotional insecurity as it is of intellectual conviction. To be rooted emotionally in "another's work of art" is to hide from the commonplace; it is to sit before the fire, not go out into the storm.

The commonplace is difficult to isolate in recall of the creative process because it is undramatically with us all the time, obvious and without glory. We tend to forget the commonplace point of departure and to recall ourselves as having started from the higher, more knowledgeable, more detached plane. When this forgetfulness is formalized into a methodology, it reinforces the rejection of the commonplace.

[1] Whitehead, A. N., *The Aims of Education* (New York: Macmillan, 1929), p. 79.

Until the early part of this century the commonplace for most human beings included the barnyard and a continuous contact with plants and animals, with everyday reminders of the biological substratum of our existence. Urban life has obviously displaced this with a man-made and mechanical commonplace. The commonplace of the past was organic and concrete; the commonplace of the present is synthetic and abstract. A horse, or cow, or a spider endures as a species. Organic functions are unfinished, cyclical, and self-reproductive. But an automobile, a washing machine, or a T.V. set is replaced with a new model. Synthetic functions are complete and more obviously subject to decay. Yet the concrete organic data of the world constitute the basis for metaphor, and the best we can do with the abstract mechanical data is to impart to them the qualities of the organic data. "The damn car won't go! It's as stubborn as a mule." The automobile came before the airplane, as the mule came before the automobile, but a pilot would never say "The damn airplane won't go! It's as stubborn as an auto."

Concrete evocative commonplace must be distinguished from abstract impotent commonplace. Fundamental originality depends on a review of the data of organic life which produced the synthetic objects and theories to which our culture is heir. To understand contemporary data and build on them without perceiving their ancestors is at best to improve—not to invent. The platform of abstract commonplace floats safely above the earth's concreteness, but we must risk abandoning it in order to grasp a more coherent creative product.

THE PROBLEM OF THE EXPERT

One way to look at group problem-solving is to consider the group as a communication network. Each individual taking part in the discussion receives messages and can also originate them. The group responds as a whole so that responses are composed by several sources. This is similar to a kind of spontaneous amplification where messages in reply to the original question are transmitted as though they emanated from a single source, when actually five or six separate individuals are pooling their communicative power. The resistance of the individual circuits must be minimized. Low resistance corresponds to high permissiveness, and this again is a characteristic of a favorable atmosphere for the synthesis of ideas.

By lowering the threshold of discrimination, a great deal of commonplace and possibly irrelevant and useless information will be communicated. The amount of "commonplace" information communicated is a measure of the lack of resistance. It is impossible to tell before hand which information is useful and which is not. An attempt to discriminate imposes on the group a censorship which atomizes it into its component parts where each individual tests his own messages before transmission, instead of all communications being parts of the same message. When an individual speaks only in a clear logical relation to the previous speech, the result is greater difficulty in synthesizing a new idea from old ones because of his inability to communicate the old ideas on a low-resistance level.

It is not only detrimental to disregard "commonplace" ideas until the leap of creative intuition has been made, but such an attitude ignores old experience which is the source of new knowledge. Although it may seem paradoxical, resistance to novelty carries with it in practice the inability to state what is partial, obvious, tentative, or wrong—in fact anything which is not final and rational. This is what commonly occurs when a group of experts gives an answer to a problem. Unless one of them is already equipped with a clever solution, the answer will take the form of a consensus of analytical opinion.

The quality of "expertness" consists of access to special knowledge of a subject which supposedly lifts the expert's thoughts out of the slough of commonness. In an analytical sense, this is true. However, when it comes to the advancement of knowledge, even within his special field, the expert is often the man least able to create a new idea, unless he is capable of suspending his expert's abstract attitude toward the subject. This attitude consists of the inability to state the commonplace (the partial, obvious, tentative, wrong). Such an attitude reveals a rigid psychological distance from the subject, rather than the *variable* and "schizophrenic" *use of distance* by the fanciful imagination. The expert tends to discuss the problem in the language of his own technology. This language can surround the problem with an impenetrable jacket so that nothing can be added or modified. The result is that it becomes impossible to view the problem in a new way . . . yet the knowledge of the expert is necessary for technical breakthrough. From nothing nothing comes.

The artist will range freely through the multiplicity of experience, selecting at will and by whim. The scientist is popularly assumed to be strictly limited by the methodology and laws of his discipline. In practice, mediocrity, not only in science but also in the arts, is characterized by narrowness of vision and concomitant rigidity of limits popularly attributed only to the scientist. Work of a fundamental and creative order in art as in science derives from the ability to range freely, continually oscillating in search of unity from multiplicity.

Highly trained people tend to have a view of the universe that is intellectualized like abstract art, but it is another's work of art which they have idealized and prefer not to fracture. They have worked hard to master their area of specialization, perhaps even suffered privation during their years of education, and they refuse to abandon these hard-won conventions. Sometimes to attack their convention is to attack the people themselves. The result is that they do not operate as individuals but as images of themselves, and this image itself is a convention. This fear of communicating as persons and insistence upon communicating as professionals rules them out from the kind of breakthroughs which derive from a deeply subjective response to a problem. An over-specialized chemist faced with a technical problem responds not as a whole man, but as a "chemical" man. He rigorously denies any part of himself except the rational and analytical.

Many times in the history of science something which has been held to be impossible was later proved to be feasible. The skeptics were locked into a way of thinking, caught in their web of familiarity. To break through toward a creative act, it is necessary to twist out of phase whatever conventional laws appear to hold. This does not mean that it is necessary to defy all the basic hypotheses of our phenomenology, but that it is necessary to defy them *apparently*. Then, through the cracks which appear when the laws are twisted out of phase (all this attained through conscious self-deceit), things can be seen in a new way. So long as the rules are accepted as immutable "laws of vision" the world always will appear to be the same and no novelties can be discovered or fabricated. Many highly trained people naturally tend to think in terms of the dogma of their own technology and it frightens them to twist their conventions out of phase. Their conventions sometimes constitute a background of knowledge upon which they rely for their emotional stability. Such experts do not want cracks to appear. They identify their psychic order with the cosmic order and any cracks are signs of their orderly cosmos breaking up.

The following transcription is edited from a session devoted to the problem of inventing a product or family of products which could grow to an annual sales potential of $300,000,000. The participants were a physical chemist, a zoologist, a physicist, a psychologist, a musician, and a man whose academic background was in English literature. The reader should be on the lookout for (a) how the scientists make strange for themselves the technical aspects as they attempt to describe these aspects in non-technical terms, (b) how the scientists resist "irresponsible" juggling of the eternal truths; (c) how the liberties taken by the non-scientists result in constructive viewpoints.

A: I'm afraid we've bitten off a big one this time . . . for us to attempt to dream up something which will yield a half a billion dollars a year gross income is some kind of cosmic impiety.

B: Maybe. Whatever we do it will have to be big. How can we make sure it will be big?

D: A do-it-yourself portable antigravity machine would have universality.

F: You mean an antigravity appliance.

D: That's right. No home would be without one.

E: That's no joke, you know. . . . Would universality of appeal derive from any product which defied a basic law?

C: Come now. You're not going to defy a basic law.

E: We could pretend to. . . . My point is that if we need universality, something big, one way of getting it is to twist a law around and develop a product based on a new way of viewing it.

C: Well, if you want to get in trouble, let's pick entropy.

D: What?

C: Entropy, the Second Law of Thermodynamics.

D: What does it mean?

C: It means that the universe is going irreversibly from order to disorder.

A: . . . and everything will finally stop.

E: I don't get it.

A: It means that if change occurs in a system the available energy in that system will decrease.

C: (goes to the board) Here's the symbolic Clausian equation. . . . (Draws) $dQ/_T + dQ^1/_{T^1} + \ldots$, or $\Sigma\,{}^{dQ}/_T$, for short

B: I thought I understood but now I'm worse off than I was before you started to clarify matters with your equations. What do they mean? Can't you explain it more simply?

A: Here, let me try. Let's say you build a road in the woods. You put down asphalt on top of gravel and so on. In other words you build order into it. As soon as your road is finished nature goes to work on it. Frost heaves buckle the asphalt and pretty soon the road is ruined. This is oversimplification, of course. But it will serve as a homey example of entropy.

F: "Something there is that doesn't love a wall,". . . is that what you're saying?

A: In a way . . . yes.

E: Things wear out . . . is that it?

C: Okay . . . your oversimplification makes me a little nervous . . . but let it pass for now.

D: Let's repeal the law of entropy.

A: Hold on a minute. I won't be a party to that kind of nonsense.

D: All right then . . . let's apparently repeal the law of entropy.

C: Go ahead.

D: I want to build a road that doesn't wear out. Is there anything that doesn't go to pot after a while?

C: Nothing I can think of.

E: Is there something that *loves* a wall . . . something that wants it to last forever?

C: Just the man who built it.

A: That's right. The man who built the wall put energy into it. Took the disorderly stones and fixed them into an orderly pattern. But unless he keeps adding energy to the system it will go towards disorder.

F: You're describing an untidy Deity.

A: That's the state of affairs. I didn't make it.

E: Doesn't anything *apparently* endure?

D: Sure. A species. In fact it grows.

C: Now don't kid yourself. Don't start thinking you have repealed the law of entropy, because you haven't.

D: Will it make you any happier if I use the word "apparently"?

C: Go ahead.

D: Species of plants and animals survive . . . even increase.

E: I see a road made up of something like coral . . . live coral. . . . As fast as the road corrodes—that's what entropy means to me, a kind of eternal corrosion—it builds itself up again.

B: What you have to do is build into the coral the wish to become a road.

E: We need synthetic coral . . . I like that "build in" business. Glue has a built-in desire to hold something together. This desire is put in at the factory and released for use when the glue is applied.

A: Can you protect the technical possibility of a material which will want to add to itself?

B: How about a foam plastic?

A: But foam plastic doesn't add to itself when necessary . . . it only can grow once.

D: So our problem is how to store the built-in suspended animation.

B: . . . the built-in training . . .

D: Same thing to me. . . . Okay.

F: Is there anything that gets frozen in ice . . . then lives when the ice thaws? Couldn't we do something like that?

C: Are you talking about something living or not?

F: Either.

C: Well, it makes a hell of a difference. If you're talking about living matter then we have the problem of synthesizing it.

E: Not only that but you're implying a production system and tradition which flies in the face of everything that has happened in the chemical industry for the past half century.

F: How come?

E: Take DuPont. . . . What does synthetic mean? It means other than organic, other than alive. Can you see their faces when you suggest that they put themselves back fifty years and start manufacturing a product which is alive? There goes their quality control.

D: Maybe. But I bet the industry of the future is an integration of the living with the nonliving.

C: I still want to decide what we are talking about right here and now. It makes a big difference.

F: I want to can plants . . . put 'em in an actual tin-can, then paint 'em on when you need them. And they will grow right where you put them. How's that?

A: I would like to hear you protect the technical feasibiilty of that one.

F: You're so busy protecting your all mighty law of entropy that you won't let me go anywhere.

A: Come on now. How will you proceed?

F: Well. I'd look for an animal or plant that was tough as hell and I'd put a bunch of them in a can and put the lid on.

B: The toughest things I know of are lichens. You see them right on top of the snow in the Arctic . . . Greenland that is.

F: You've got something there. Let's can lichens. Paint them on a wall and we're in business.

D: Does anyone here really know about lichens? What they really are I mean? . . . Then let's look them up in the Britannica. . . . I'll be darned. Lichens are part algae and part fungi . . . with a symbiotic relationship between the two.

C: How do they reproduce?

D: It says here lichens get their nutrition from the atmosphere and that they can live where neither a fungus or the algae could live alone.

C: How do they reproduce?

D: Wait a minute. It says you can sow lichen spores, must be the seeds, and the right algae on a sterile glass plate and that they will grow . . . growth is speeded up by the use of a nutritive solution. My God there are all sorts of colors and sizes . . . take your pick.

A: None of us is qualified in this area.

E: Right, but let's check into the matter a little further.

B: What would they be used for anyway?

F: Instead of paint. Paint wears out but lichen paint would go on forever.

B: Where would you paint them then?

F: Houses.

A: The wood would rot.

F: In that case don't use wooden houses.

D: You know where they'd be great? Cement block houses. . . .
As it is, cement block is second class construction. A lovely organic
growth would make a cement block house have all the old world appeal of an English cottage. Hey! . . . Here's the poop on reproduction.
The spore form of lichens is called soredia. As spores they're even
tougher than the lichens themselves.

F: If they are tougher then let's can them!

B: Where else would you want lichens?

E: Road dividers. Today they're using grass as road dividers on the
big super highways. With grass you need loam, if it's dry you have to
water artificially and after all that you have to cut the grass. The grass
gets you coming and going.

D: That's not such a dumb idea. Listen to this. "In states of great
cold or great heat or great deprivation in general, lichens endure by
suspending growth". . . but they do not die.

B: And you wouldn't have to cut them the way you do grass.
They would take care of themselves and always look tidy. . . .

A: What we have to do is get hold of someone who knows lichens
and get him to help us design an experiment to prove that we can get
decent growth from some kind of culture.

C: This use of lower plants gives me an idea. . . . You know,
there are hundreds of desolate areas in the world—desert areas that is—
dust bowls. Nothing will grow. They try to plant hardy little trees and
the trees die. Here's my idea. Take your canned lower plant "seeds"
with the nutrient in them—plants that will flourish from deriving their
nutrition from the atmosphere—plants like lichens. Spray these all over
and you know what? You will be remaking the botanical world the
natural way, the way it was made in the first place. You'll be starting
with primitive plants—then more sophisticated plants—later there will
be a little natural humus and so on. Only with your special nutrient you
can speed up the process so that it will be effective. . . .

F: You can play God!

A: I like that notion. But let me state again we have not defied entropy—not at all.

This research is under way. The expert believed that it was possible to can the soredial forms of lichens and suggested a variety of experiments to initiate the project. Since then new markets have presented themselves which include the canning of such lower plants as mosses to serve as substitutes for grass, the notion being to spray this living paint on patios, etc. The concept of "living paint" has matured so that it is now contemplated that the product will consist of the soredia, nutrient, dye (to give the appearance of cover immediately) and an adhesive. But more important than the product is the interplay of the diverse people who contributed to the concept. The "experts" in entropy first made the strange familiar to the others. Then the efforts of the others to understand resulted in metaphors and comparisons which led to a constructive viewpoint.

"I told him that we had better go a little further in the analysis of the problem ourselves before we tried to get in any specialists, because they would make the problem conform to known facts."[2] Practical men, even inventors, view the contribution of experts as limited. Synectics, however, takes into account the great potential contribution of experts as well as the difficulty of making use of it. In Synectics sessions even the most specialized expert can be the person best fitted for comparing the problem as understood with the analogies and metaphors produced by the use of mechanisms. His function can be seen from the following:

A: Dr. E, we are lucky to have you join us for a little while this morning. We do not feel that we are qualified in the area implied by the problem we are trying to get a handle on.

E: Perhaps I'll be a disappointment.

A: I don't think so. B, why don't you give Dr. E the poop?

[2] Boyd, T. A., *Charles Franklin Kettering* (New York: E. P. Dutton, 1957), p. 57.

B: Okay. We have been given the assignment to develop a paint which will cling to the chalky surface of a house. Apparently the chalky residue of the previous paint jobs makes repainting a tough job. The new paint peels off too soon.

A: Dr E, we simply don't know enough about the chemistry of paints to judge the possibility of success about any concept we get.

E: I've heard a lot about how you gentlemen operate . . . Synectics I think you call it . . . but you'd better fill me in.

A: About fifteen years ago we began to develop a theory about how the creative process operates. Over the years we have broken down the process into mechanisms by which we evoke creative viewpoints which can result in solutions to problems. These mechanisms are made up of various kinds of analogies to the problem at hand . . . they constitute potential new ways of looking at the problems.

C: But when we are dealing with a technological area which is unfamiliar to us we have to bring in someone who can evaluate the pertinence of our conceptual associations to the problem.

A: That's right. We would like to throw a whole bunch of associations at you and have you flip them onto the problem and judge whether there is anything useful in the new ways of looking at the problem as we go along.

E: You mean you want me to tell you if your solutions will work?

A: Not exactly . . . Look. Why don't we just get started and you plug in as we go along . . . all right? D, can you summon up a Direct Analogy to this paint thing?

D: I think of the chalky surface as being a duck's back . . . the water or paint falls off.

E: Why?

D: Why what?

E: Why does water fall right off a duck's back?

D: Because the duck has oil or something on his feathers that makes his back impervious to water.

B: Dr. E, would you say that paint refuses to stick to the chalky surface in the same way water falls off a duck's back?

E: Not exactly. A duck's back is hydrophobic and the water particles remain in droplets and thus do not penetrate. As you say, "they fall off." The chalky residue of paint on the side of a house is easily "wetted" by new paint. The trouble is that the new paint doesn't get through to the subsurface. As the polymer wears away it leaves behind it the poorly bonded filler . . . clay or any number of things.

C: What would be ideal here is to open up a can of paint, throw it against a wall and have the paint "want" to spread itself around evenly.

E: Yes. That would be ideal. How would you do it?

C: Who knows? You'd have to build into the paint, at the factory, an affinity for wood.

D: And you'd have to build in another "wish" . . . a wish to be evenly spread.

B: Can you do anything with that, Dr. E?

E: Not really . . . it's too far out for me.

D: All right. Let's come at Dr. E with another one.

B: I'm a drop of paint and I've just been put on a chalky surface. I don't like the chalky surface because I know I can only make a temporary home for myself there. I'm in a panic. I'm falling, falling. I try to reach through the subsurface, but I can't. I'm slipping, slipping. I'm going to fall . . . to be killed. I'm scratching with my claws to find a decent hold on the subsurface. But I'm slipping by. Faster and faster! I can't get through to the good holding stuff. . . .

A: What can you do with that, Dr. E?

E: I'm intrigued with it . . . the 'claws' particularly. You see, if the chalky surface were brushed, just so there would not be little pieces of chalkiness sticking up . . . if this could be done, and I think it would be economical, you might put a solvent in with the paint. The ideal would be for the solvent to pierce through the chalky surface, like B's claws, and for the paint to follow the solvent through to the under-surface.

A: Can you expand on that?

E: I am just speculating, but it may be an interesting way to look at the problem. . . . The solvent, let's call the vehicle that pierces through to the undersurface a solvent for now . . . the solvent might get through, but it would not be adhesive. The question is how to get the polymer through and how to polymerize the old paint . . . the un-bonded chalky residue . . . hmmm. Maybe . . . your "claws" would be the solvent. . . .

From the above one can see that the expert was able to use the analogies which were offered him, particularly the "claws" analogy. The other members of the group did not have the special knowl-edge to consider what the analogy meant in technical terms. Also the expert assisted in illuminating the problem as understood. No attempt was made to force the expert to abandon his specialist's role, so he didn't feel at all threatened; in fact he was amused by and in-terested in the group's performance. Afterward the chemist who participated in the session outlined above confessed that he had been moved by B's predicament in two ways. In the first place he found himself identified along with B with the droplet of paint which was falling to its "death." In the second place he became sympathetic toward B who seemed to feel that he, B, were sharing the same fate as the droplet—but as a person, not a droplet.

If an expert spends much time with a Synectics group he begins to pick up the technique of the mechanisms and contribute to sessions. But it is dangerous to try to influence him in this direction unless he asks. In setting up Synectics groups for clients, those technical peo-ple are chosen who appear, from our interview with them, to have a tendency toward the use of mechanisms. In fact a major part of our interviewing technique is the use of the mechanisms as a test of the people whom we choose for the client group.

THE COMMONPLACE AS METAPHOR

Highly trained technical people often think in terms of the im-mutable validity of their own special technology. They resist twisting their conventions out of phase. Yet acceptance of old rules as a "law of vision" denies the possibility of basic novelty. Conventions as abstractions from reality constitute a virtually complete and unassailable pattern, whereas the commonplace is infinitely repatternable. Since conventions are orderly ways of considering and making palatable the infinite data of the commonplace, it can be emotionally traumatic to abandon the security of this order in favor of the disorderly commonplace. Thus there is built into the human mind a resistance to the study of the commonplace. This resistance can be overcome best by skilful use of metaphor.

Metaphor is usually considered from its verbal manifestations; and in fact verbal metaphor does offer a rich accessible field for initial investigation. However, most metaphors underlying traditional individualistic invention occur as vague images or emerge into verbal form only after-the-fact of the original synthesis. An exclusively literary approach would be far too limited for Synectics. It is essential to distinguish between metaphor which is decorative and after-the-fact (in that it does not discover but describes the already-discovered) and metaphor which is generative, inductive, before-the-fact—the initial leap in the process of discovery.

Metaphor is an expressed or implied comparison which produces simultaneously meaningful intellectual illumination and emotional excitement. The most familiar cases of metaphor are analogy and simile. Both give us insight through explicit comparison, usually with "as" or "like" in their syntax. Analogy seems logical or scientific since it focuses on a similarity of relations or of function. An atom is *like* a solar system because the *relations* of electrons in orbit around a nucleus are analogous to the *relations* of the planets in orbit around the sun. On the other hand, in terms of like function, analogy could hold that a piston pump was *like* a centrifugal pump in that both are pumps.

General analogy illuminates demonstrable points of similarity and is widely used in the description and explanation of scientific and logical ideas. Simile, on the other hand, is a more poetic order of comparison. It also uses the overt reminder "like" or "as": "My love is *like* a red, red rose." But here, opposed to analogy, the emphasis is not on similarity but on the excitement which is generated when two relatively unlike things ("my love" and a "red, red rose") have qualities attributed to each other.

Simile shares with metaphor a two-directional motion. It does not simply attribute the qualities of the *rose* to *my love* but also refines the *rose* in the light of its connection with *my love*. Simile, like metaphor is not complete. Not all possible points of connection are intended to hold. It is left to our minds to complete the connection.

This encourages us to see and feel much or little, depending upon our richness of association, thus opening the possibility of putting our preconscious minds to work. Simile also requires a discriminating response; not all possible points of bearing are intended to hold. The *rose-love* connection is not supposed to mean that her face is red. But in spite of this ambivalence, simile, like analogy, tends to strike us as logical because it is explicitly comparative. It is "safer" than a metaphor which flatly equates unlike objects or states. To say: "Life is *like* a river," is less daring than the direct statement: "Life is a river." Simile emphasizes areas of "differentness" rather than areas of sameness of the things being compared. The intention of the statement: "Life is like a river" is restrained. Life is, of course, not a river, but there are some points of similarity (the motion of flow, passage through time, etc.) which bear comparison.

"The ship plows over the sea." Here, by implication, the ship's prow is *like* a plow; the wave pattern of the sea is *like* the furrowed pattern of plowed ground, and the whole motion of the ship is associated with the purposiveness implied by plowing. Two opposing things happen in these metaphors of direct and indirect equation: we are asked to link points of similarity between dissimilar things —shape and motion of prow and plow, visual pattern of sea and plowed ground, and the more abstract idea of productivity—and we are asked to leave out or look past all the points of dissimilarity which, incidentally, contribute excitement and tension by holding ship-sea and plow-land apart even as they are being spoken of as similar. This type of metaphor forces us to float many variables and gives the mind many opportunities to select associations which can lead to new insights.

Within the potentialities of metaphor are two extremes (with all the gradations in between). At one extreme is the metaphor comparing entities that enjoy a high degree of likeness, with only minor differentiations to distinguish between them. We say that an atom is like a little solar system to accentuate the degree of likeness. At this extreme, minor unlikenesses prevent the comparison from being an actual identity.

At the opposite end of the spectrum, metaphor can open the mind to comparison between entities which enjoy practically no likeness to each other, where the actual point of contact is almost fantastic. To say that a thrush's egg looks like "a little low heaven" compares visual similarities (color and arched shape) which constitute a tenuous point of contact between radically unlike things. At this extreme the comprehension of the metaphor forces the point of relationship; if the metaphor works, this apparently tenuous point becomes a pivot upon which the two realms of the unlike swing toward a momentary coalescence: for a moment the thrush's egg can give us the feeling of a heaven in its entirety.

A different sort of metaphor can be described as empathic. It involves us personally and gives us a new feeling about or understanding of an object of state. Anthropomorphization and personification are examples of this kind of metaphor. Anthropomorphization is the attribution of human characteristics to non-human things or states. Personification is less inclusive; it represents an object or an abstract idea as endowed with human attribute. Thus, if we say about a valve that it "wants" to close, we attribute to the valve the ability *to want*. Empathic metaphor is, however, more inclusive than these two examples would indicate. The basic questions which suggest this inclusiveness are: "How would I feel if I were. . . ." or "What would it say to me if it could think, respond, and talk the way I can?" Essentially this sort of metaphor involves an achievement of identification-with where the person retains his own self-consciousness as the basis of comparison. To lose this self-consciousness in total identification would, of course, eliminate the evocative power of the metaphor by losing the point of comparison.

To understand the function of metaphor in the creative process we must see how metaphor is used *after* as well as *before* the fact. Metaphor functions prior to the moment of breakthrough and during the achievement of original synthesis. Metaphor is *generative* or *inductive* as well as decorative or descriptive. The *before-the-fact* order of metaphor is far more difficult to get at because, being prior to "discovery," it gets lost or buried beneath layers of self-conscious autobiography in both artist and scientist.

A generative approach, though not precisely aimed at true or specifically demonstrable states, is Thoreau's attempt to perceive the essential unity of the natural world. In "Natural History of Massachusetts" he begins a metaphoric sequence with the initial perception that ice crystals on a stalk in winter are like leaves in summer:

"Every tree, shrub and spire of grass, that could raise its head above the snow, was covered with a dense ice-foliage, answering, as it were, leaf for leaf to its summer dress."[3]

Thoreau then proceeds to expand speculatively this original and metaphoric perception of the similarity between dissimilar objects and states:

". . . It struck me that these ghost leaves, and the green ones whose forms they assume, were the creatures of but one law; that in obedience to the same law the vegetable juices swell gradually into the perfect leaf, on the one hand, and the crystalline particles troop to their standards in the same order on the other. As if the material were indifferent, but the law one and invariable. . . . This foliate structure is common to the coral and the plumage of birds, and to how large a part of animate and inanimate nature. . . ."[4]

Thoreau goes on to see comparable "crystalline structure" in "fields waving with grain," in "high towering palms," and "arctic pines"—in fissured mud, asbestos, and quartz (which he calls "the

[3] Thoreau, Henry David, *The Portable Thoreau*, ed. Carl Bode, (New York: Viking, 1947), p. 52.
[4] *Ibid.*, p. 53.

frostwork of a longer night.") The net result of this metaphoric extension is not so much a "scientific truth" as it is the "conceptual truth" that nature functions in terms of order and pattern (crystals) and that this function cuts across the traditional line separating animate from inanimate realms. What generates this sequence is the recognition of the visual analogue of ice crystals and leaves, two commonplace phenomena which only relate by "accident," apart from the metaphoric insight which momentarily unites them.

Another sort of generative metaphor is described by Thoreau in *Walden:*

"While I was surveying, the ice, which was sixteen inches thick, undulated under a slight wind like water. It is well known that a level cannot be used on ice. At one rod from the shore its greatest fluctuation, when observed by means of a level on land directed toward a graduated staff on the ice, was three quarters of an inch, though the ice appeared firmly attached to the shore. It was probably greater in the middle. Who knows but if our instruments were delicate enough we might detect an undulation in the crust of the earth?"[5]

Clearly this metaphor works by analogy, from a measurable known (the undulation of pond ice) to an unknown (the undulation of the earth's crust). Underlying the analogy is the equation: The ice crust is over liquid (water) as the earth's crust is over liquid (molten core). Thoreau cultivated a metaphoric habit of mind and sought to dramatize that mode of seeing as the primary mode of perception, the primary mode of what he called being "awake" as against being "blind" or "asleep." Consequently he made a consistent autobiographical attempt to record and clarify his own processes of perception, and in his writings the process is more important than the end product. He taught himself to be metaphorical, and Synectics theory is based on the capacity of people to learn this metaphorical attitude of mind. The use of metaphor is a characteristic of man. Though hidden and inhibited in some people, Synectics re-

[5] *Ibid.,* pp. 533–534.

search reveals that there are certain practical psychological conditions for its re-emergence as a useful tool for human invention.

Most "scientific" metaphors function primarily as a realization of the unknown in terms of the known, or of the unimaginable in terms of the imaginable.

The physicist George Gamow reports that his discoveries of the play of force within an atomic nucleus derived from his assumption "that the material of the atomic nucleus is built along the same lines as any ordinary liquid."[6] The coherence of the nucleus, he thought, might be understood in terms of surface tension, etc.—by direct analogy to the coherence of a droplet of water. Thus, the generative metaphor postulates an identity between the known, graspable, everyday droplet of water and the unknown, elusive atomic nucleus. This identity is essentially relational and has about it an aura of excitement because it is potentially informative and "new." The next developmental phase through which the metaphor passes (and in terms of which it is refined) is essentially logical, deriving the implications of the metaphor by logic, mathematics, or by additional developmental metaphor. In this phase the relational aptness of the metaphor is tested, its implications expanded and checked. If the mathematical descriptions of surface tension in a droplet of water fit the data about the properties of the nucleus (and they seem to), then the metaphor expands toward an inclusiveness which we call "true."

Our capacity to use language has been dulled and the consequence is a limitation of ability to grasp new relationships.[7] Contemporary theory about language holds that language is essentially metaphorical in its nature and development. This theory is grounded in the school of neurophysiology which maintains that symbolization is an inherent function of the nervous system, that the nervous system does

[6] Gamow, George, *One, Two, Three—Infinity* (New York: Viking, 1947), p. 160.

[7] Bronowski, J., *The Common Sense of Science* (Cambridge. Mass.: Harvard University Press, 1953), p. 11.

not return direct impressions of the external world but indirect symbolical representations. This position further maintains that the rudimentary symbolization process of the nervous system is elaborated on higher and higher levels, culminating in the brain.

When this argument is extended, language is asserted to have its roots in metaphor and through metaphor in the rich, symbol-making earth of the nervous system itself. "Metaphor is a law of growth of every semantic. It is not a development but a principle."[8] Thus language does not originate or develop in primarily utilitarian terms but in terms of metaphor; and in this sense words develop by metaphoric extension. The word "bridge" for example, meant originally "a plank"; subsequently the plank's various uses expanded into the present meaning of the word, and even that meaning has a whole cluster of traditional metaphoric uses—so traditional that we are not conscious of making a metaphor when we speak of "bridging the gap" between the arts and the sciences or between east and west.

Another and more subtle example is buried in a word like *electric*. It derives from the Greek word *elektron* which meant *amber* and was linked with the Greek *elektor* which means *gleaming* or *the beaming sun*. Electricity then, first made or associated with the friction of amber, picked up its name and some of its associations from amber.[9] By the late eighteenth century it would be defined as "a property in some bodies, whereby when rubbed so as to grow warm, they draw little bits of paper, or such like substance, to them" (Dr. Johnson). And it is not until well into the nineteenth century that the familiar uses of the word evolve, including the common metaphoric meaning of exciting or thrilling.

Language is a vast repository of "faded metaphors" i.e., words originally used in a metaphoric sense which have now acquired the abstract or relational meaning they first metaphorically suggested. It

[8] Langer, Suzanne, *Philosophy in a New Key* (Cambridge, Mass.: Harvard University Press, 1951), p. 119.

[9] For a further discussion of the evolution of words via metaphoric extension, cf Owen Barfield, *History in English Words* (London: Methuen, 1926).

is this concept of language as inherently metaphoric that leads Suzanne Langer to remark: "(metaphor) is the force that makes (language) essentially relational, intellectual, forever showing up new, abstractable forms in reality."[10] Thus metaphor as a mental principle (inherent in language and grounded in the nervous system) is essential to the endeavour to grasp new relationships and to the ability to comprehend generality.

These speculations are borne out in studies of a child's approach to a grasp of language. "There are strong reasons for presuming that primitive child language fulfills far more complicated functions than would at first appear to be the case."[11] In fact the child begins directly to exploit the non-utilitarian aspects of language. Language interests the child as an incredibly useful way of inventing new relationships, of putting the world together. It is fun in itself—an elaborate and yet real game which enables the child to grasp on higher levels those relationships which his nervous system continually produces. It enables the child to move from the known into the unknown and to approach the comprehension of those higher levels of generality analogous to the generalizations which the nervous system synthesizes into sense impressions. A striking instance of the failure of the utilitarian theory of language occurred in the teaching of Helen Keller. Attempts to teach her to speak were uniformly unsuccessful. She could not be taught to say "water" but finally learned the word, her first, when her hand was plunged in a cold, moving stream of water. This initial awareness of words was kinesthetic and relational, involving temperature and motion rather than use; and thus, in a rudimentary sense, it was metaphoric rather than utilitarian.

Once language is understood as fundamentally metaphoric, its relational potential can be expanded in a variety of ways—not only by making new metaphors but by revitalizing the old and faded. The

10 Langer, Suzanne, op. cit., p. 115.
11 Piaget, Jean, The Language and Thought of the Child (New York: Meridian Books, 1955), p. 28.

utilitarian and logical functions of language then come to be regarded as secondary, i.e., not generative of new relations but descriptive of traditional and established relations. Nor is this fact true simply of words; it can be expanded to include all other forms of language. Mathematics is, in this sense, primarily a relational game which secondarily can be converted to utilitarian functions. The same is true of languages that involve visual relationships as in painting, for example, or sound-relationships as in music. This discussion of words (the most completely developed and most comprehensive language humanity has evolved) should be taken as a case in point and not as comprehending all the reaches of metaphor.

Discovery and invention in mathematics and physics are particularly rich in non-verbal generative metaphor, and yet the non-verbal nature of the metaphor frequently gives rise to a certain obscurity in the reports and interpretations of these experiences. The French mathematician Hadamard says about words and algebraic signs, "whenever the matter looks more difficult, they become too heavy a baggage for me. I use concrete representations . . ."

Hadamard then gives some examples of such concrete representations—"spots of undefined form," points massed and strung out by various schemes, etc.—which he calls "strange and cloudy imagery."

"One can easily realize how such a mechanism or an analogous one may be necessary for me for the understanding of the . . . proof [that the sequel of prime numbers is unlimited]. I need it in order to have a simultaneous view of all elements of the argument, to hold them together, to make a whole of them . . ."[12]

The element of playful impracticality is repeatedly emphasized in autobiographical accounts of scientific discovery and fits as corollary to the double assertion that (a) language is essentially metaphoric and playful and only secondarily utilitarian; and (b) the child's grasp of language is initially playful and only latterly utilitarian. In general these autobiographical accounts suffer from an unanalytic emphasis on "moments of inspiration" or "apparent sudden illumi-

[12] Hadamard, Jacques, *The Psychology of Invention in the Mathematical Field* (Princeton: Princeton University Press, 1945), pp. 75–76.

nation." Analytically, however, these "moments" emerge as (1) devoid of practical behavior (i.e. play or reverie) and (2) characterized by some sort of metaphoric conjunction.

The Dutch physicist Kekule described the birth of the structural theory of the atom in these terms;

"One beautiful summer evening I was riding on the last omnibus through the deserted streets usually so filled with life. I rode as usual on the outside of the omnibus. I fell into a reverie. Atoms flitted before my eyes. I had never before succeeded in perceiving their manner of moving. That evening, however, I saw that frequently two smaller atoms were coupled together, that larger ones seized the two smaller ones, that still larger ones held fast three and even four of the smaller ones and that all were whirled around in a bewildering dance. I saw how the larger atoms formed a row and one dragged along still smaller ones at the ends of the chain. . . . The cry of the guard, 'Clapham Road,' waked me from my reverie; but I spent a part of the night writing down sketches of these dream pictures. Thus arose the structural theory."[13]

Here the two conditions, non-practical behavior and metaphoric play are clearly stated as they are in another of Kekule's reminiscences, this time about the discovery of the benzene ring:

". . . I turned my chair toward the fireplace and sank into a doze. Again the atoms were flitting before my eyes. Smaller groups now kept modestly in the background. My mind's eye sharpened by repeated visions of a similar sort, now distinguished larger structures of varying forms. Long rows frequently rose together, all in movement, winding and turning like serpents; and see! What was that? One of the serpents seized its own tail and the form whirled mockingly before my eyes. I came awake like a flash of lightning. This time also I spent the remainder of the night working out the consequences of the hypothesis."[14]

Edison's invention of the phonograph has strangely similar conditions: it derived from a "toy" and from the analogue of the motions of a paper man and sound vibrations:

[13] Libby, Walter, "The Scientific Imagination," *Scientific Monthly,* XV (1922), pp. 263–270.
[14] *Ibid.*

". . . Edison created the phonograph in a single day in 1877. Years before . . . a phenomenon occurred while he was experimenting upon the idea of sending a telegraph signal from a whirling disc upon which a stylus pricked electromagnetic embossed telegraphic dots and dashes, creating a musical hum when the disc whirled at high speed. In 1877 he developed a funnel-like toy. When he talked through the funnel, the vibrations caused by his voice worked a pawl which turned a ratchet wheel connected by a pulley with a paper figure of a man operating a paper saw on a paper log. Edison noted that at times the man moved rhythmically, at times jerkily, depending upon the words shouted at the horn and the pitch of his voice. Out of the setting of the musical hum, noted years previously, and the industrious paper man sawing his paper log came the *flash of insight* which produced a phonograph in thirty hours."[15]

The simple substitution of the words "the metaphoric conjunction" for "the flash of insight" makes clear the process of synthesis by which contemplation of the commonplace underlies inventive viewpoint.

SUMMARY

Generative metaphors seem to take their inception in essentially subliminal process—a process of which we are not thoroughly conscious at the moment of its occurrence. Thus, we tend to slide past the moment of inception, to regard it as mysterious and sacrosanct, to call it inspiration, and to overlook the possible effects of training and discipline upon the metaphor-making potential. However, even a good descriptive metaphor has a quality of "mystery" about it as it postulates similarities between apparently unlike things, and as it illuminates and excites in the "confusion" of our impressions by simultaneously suggesting an identity (a similarity) and a separateness (a dissimilarity). This quality of mystery then is present in both descriptive and generative metaphors, though to different de-

[15] Porterfield, Austin L., *Creative Factors in Scientific Research* (Durham: Duke University, 1941), p. 95.

grees. The impression of mystery may derive from the fact that a metaphoric sort of activity operates not only on conscious but also on preconscious and subconscious levels. This activity may describe the coordinating function of the nervous system as a whole. Perhaps the body is metaphoric. If so, training the individual to understand and celebrate metaphor (in poetry and in literature as well as in science) and training the individual to make metaphors (even though they are generally descriptive) is training him in habits of mind consonant with the functional principles of the underlevels of brain and nervous system.

According to Synectics theory the conscious attempt to make metaphors has a stimulating effect upon subliminal abilities to metaphorize in contrast to the apparently depressive effect that "utilitarian" and "logical" preoccupations have upon those abilities. Thus through the use of the operational mechanisms the "expert" can learn metaphorically to draw on the richness of the commonplace world of his own concrete perception. "Experts" who are brilliantly productive in their chosen fields have learned to use the commonplace subconsciously. "Experts" who are inhibited by the image of themselves as professionals, viewing themselves as being above the naive consideration of the commonplace, must enter a conscious didactic phase in order to take advantage of their productive potential.

The mere "innocence" of the amateur is not sufficient basis for technical problem solving and in Synectics the expert plays an indispensable role. In his analytical capacity he acts as the major source of making the strange familiar. The expert knows the familiar facts and can expound them to clarify the details and implication of a problem. In his synthetic capacity, through the use of metaphor, he can operate in two ways: 1) the expert can join the amateurs in "play," in the use of the mechanisms. This activity is particularly valuable when, for instance, an expert in biology develops biological analogies to a problem in physics; 2) the expert in the scientific field implied by the problem as understood is in the best intellectual position to compare the metaphors and analogies (produced by the use of the mechanisms with the problem as understood). This role, in Synectics, is like that of a policeman who directs the traffic of associations to the problem as understood. The results of the use of the mechanism are examined and judged on their value in illuminating the problem as understood. If a new viewpoint is attained, then this viewpoint is analyzed. If no viewpoint is forthcoming then the policeman permits the flow of associations to continue. In this way, through metaphor, the expert can make efficient and creative use of the commonplace.

In Synectics theory, play with apparent irrelevancies is used extensively to generate energy for problem-solving and to evoke new viewpoints with respect to problems. Play generates energy because it is a pleasure in itself, an intrinsic end. Kant's notions about the intrinsic value of art viewed as play without purpose[1] evoked in Schiller the hypothesis that art derives from "pure play" and excess energy.[2] The lion roars in play. His cup runneth over. He hears his own roar and enjoys the sound. The roar is an end in itself. According to Schiller, the feeling of extra power and freedom of man is expressed through art with no pragmatic overtones.[3]

Von Lange accepted the surplus energy theory of Schiller adding the notion of illusion through which, for instance, the imagination of a child at play enables him to transcend the limitations of everyday reality. The child's dreams of the Wild West transform the living room fireplace into a stable, a chair into a cow pony, and a toy pistol into a deadly forty-four. For Von Lange, play is the art of childhood, and art is the mature form of play. Both are forms of conscious self-deception with the play-acting make-believe of childhood evolving into the more controlled illusions of the adult creator.

In play and art, pleasure is not dependent upon the purpose of the activity. Expanding this axiom to include all creative activity implies that in play and *in all creative activity* the process itself is satisfying. This hypothesis, tested in practice within the various Synectics groups and checked by interviews with artists and scientists, has been verified. While it may be true that final sanction for artist, scientist, inventor is public acceptance of the end-product,

[1] Kant, Immanuel, *Critique of Judgment,* tr. J. C. Meredith (New York: Oxford University Press, 1928). Part I, Section 3, essay 45.

[2] Schiller, Friedrich, *Letters and Essays* (Boston: Little Brown, 1845), pp. 65, 72, 113.

[3] *Ibid.,* pp. 139–140.

overemphasis on the success goal masks the gratification in the creative process itself. Synectics theory implies that not all play is creative but that all creativity contains play.[4]

"Play" in the creative process means the activity of floating and considering associations *apparently* irrelevant to the problem at hand. Play in this sense involves the constructive use of illusion, conscious self-deceit, daydreams, and of associations in general which seem to imply no immediate benefit. For many years estheticians and psychologists have recognized the importance of the role of play in art. The painter plays with diverse ways of expressing on canvas what he sees with his eyes or his mind until he illuminates his own understanding of what he wants to create. However, the kinship between art and play has been overemphasized whereas the kinship between play and all forms of creative adult behavior has been overlooked. Play-theorists tend to neglect such human activities as scientific research and invention. This is a strange omission since it is obvious that children's play is technical as well as purely imaginative. A child builds up his blocks to make a bridge and a moment later he is pretending he is a cowboy. A child's every experimental exercise is an invention; it just happens that there is an abundance of prior art. The child reinvents post and lintel construction with his blocks. This kind of play is not considered technical and inventive because post and lintel construction is an old and obvious structure from the adult point of view. The adult mind has grown beyond the inventive, form-making nature of the child's play.

A child digs a tunnel in the sand and supports the tunnel wall with leaves and sticks. He makes a waterfall by detouring a rivulet. He improvises toy boats out of pine cones and sails them down the stream. It is "child's play," but it indicates a primitive sensitivity to volume displacement, gravity, and hydraulic flow. It is also form-making, involving inventive solutions to small technical prob-

[4] Gordon, William J. J., "The Role of Irrelevance in Art and Invention," paper delivered at the Third Arden House Conference on Creative Process, Nov. 1–4, 1957.

lems. It is also illusionary. A world-which-is-not is created in which
pine cones are boats and a rivulet is the Congo.

Karl Groos found in animals the same kind of conscious self-
deceit play that children enjoy. He uncovered three phases of in-
stinctive animal activity: (1) hereditary propensity—the young
puppy automatically snaps at the finger tapped on its nose; (2)
serious practice—one young dog seizes another dog's throat in
practical play; and (3) conscious play—a mature dog mouths his
master's hand in a make-believe attack and growls menacingly.
Human art, according to Groos, is the result of this kind of play
augmented by the desire to exercise power over matter by subduing
it to artistic purposes.[5] Groos does not go so far, but Synectics
maintains that the process of technical invention is the same as art.
Conscious play, integrated with a desire for power over matter and
pleasure at overcoming resistance, leads to technical inventions.

Groos adopts Souriau's concept of the hedonic satisfaction in
movements that overcome resistance.[6] "The rapid horizontal movement, the leap, the forward motion of a swing are a mock (conscious self-deceit) victory over the force of gravitation."[7] The men
prominent in the development of the airplane had to have the
imagination to "mock gravitation." In fact, the airplane is a make-
believe anti-gravitation machine. Groos and other psychologists
identify play with art to the exclusion of technical invention. Yet, it
is obvious that the example of a "mock victory over the force of
gravitation" describes an ideal area for technical invention. Before
reduction to practice, all inventions are mere illusions. The practical
implementation of these illusions is motivated among other things by
a desire for power over "the way things are" through imagining
"the way things are *not*."

The fabrication (through play) of a world that "is not" can derive
directly from a "repeal of law." Imagine a world where the inverse

[5] Groos, Karl, *The Play of Animals*, tr. Elizabeth Baldwin (New York:
Appleton-Century, 1898), chap. Art and Play.
[6] *Ibid.*
[7] Groos, Karl, *op. cit., loc. cit.*

square law does not hold, where energy can be transmitted entire over any distance from point to point. Tipping the world upside-down affects the creative process in several different ways. An initial playful speculation about a world that "is-not" extends the imagination via the necessity of completing this world. This "new" world offers a new angle of vision on the old world order. The deathless absolute of the old world order becomes relative and reformable. Most of the concepts with which humans work have been handed down pre-packaged; and we are expected to obey their authority. Creating a world in which these concepts do not hold forces us to act with a maker's responsibility rather than an inheritor's passive acceptance. This attitude of active responsibility in turn modifies our view of the "real world" whose pre-packaged ruling concepts lose their stultifying authority.

At times, this attempt to fabricate an upside-down world (a kingdom of misrule) can have more serious overtones, as when we try, for example, to understand and to define "weightlessness." In the condition of space travel, weightlessness is difficult to imagine because the human sense of orientation from birth (if not within the womb itself) is closely bound up with a sense of weight.[8] A world in which weight does not exist threatens our basic psychophysical sense of order. Nevertheless, the imaginative game of conceiving this weightlessness world is in part "play"—creating and trying to complete a world in some way opposite to our own—as a child can create in the middle of the living-room floor a ship's bridge, a frontier ranch, or a battle. We shall see how difficult it is for the average human adult to view the world as "it-is-not," how important this view is for all invention, and the operational mechanisms by which this view can be attained.

Play, as an attitude of mind and an ability on an adult level, is a direct analogue of the child's attitudes and abilities. It operates in terms of the adult individual's willingness to recall and to re-enter the child state. While adult play is commonly regarded as un-

[8] Gesell, Arnold, *The First Five Years of Life* (New York: Harper, 1940).

conscious (or regressive), for the purposes of analyzing and evoking the creative process, Synectics believes play can be disciplined and directed at will. Play in this sense involves the willingness to manipulate words, concepts, everyday and technical assumptions, together with playing with apparently irrelevant objects and things. Play in adults as in children is not merely a vacation. It is not merely a light-hearted waste of time, but another order of constructive effort constituting in itself a serious, form-making endeavour.

By "apparently irrelevant" we mean those observations, facts, generalizations, and feelings which, in accordance with accepted practice and theories, do not seem "relevant" to the problem at hand. The negative response, "that is irrelevant," is, of course, a handy way to narrow and focus a problem. Unfortunately it also means the rejection, as foreign and extraneous, of the rich potential of metaphoric and analogic associations. The ability and willingness to use the apparently irrelevant imply a redefinition of what constitutes relevancy. The tendency in both art and science, as well as in everyday experience, is to define the relevant in the narrowest, almost legalistic sense, because superficially at least, the narrow limits offer a more comprehensible working position. Some finite part of the universe must be bitten off in order for it to be considered and examined. However, Synectics research into the creative process itself reveals that those individuals (and groups) who are willing to defer this narrowing action are more imaginative and productive than individuals or groups who rapidly narrow the field.

PLAY WITH WORDS AND SYSTEMS

Play with words and phrases and their meanings and play with logical systems and patterns—as ways of making the familiar strange —are tributary to the use of the operational mechanisms of Synectics. Language (words and their extensions through grammar and syntax) is, of course, fundamental to the human ability to transpose image into symbol. It is the primary systematic means of ordering, communicating, and dealing with our experience of the world. Words, however exciting they may be at first discovery, go flat with use, becoming mechanical tags for the all-too-familiar. Language is a vast repository of petrified metaphors. To be evocative it requires periodic renewal and reinvigoration.

Play with words invigorates language and by implication re-invigorates perception as well as the way conceptions are formed. It re-establishes the wide range of metaphoric suggestiveness inherent not only in language as a whole but also in single words and phrases. We have all experienced the ways in which words, flatly employed as the name for things, are made to dispel the strange. The child who asks: "What's that funny noise?" is told the noise is thunder in such a way that speculation is supposed to stop. That weird phenomena of sourceless sound is supposed to become as safe and acceptable as the everyday tap of a hammer. But naming the noise does not describe it. It does not answer the question, it kills it. Play with language not only livens metaphor, it also involves an oscillation between particulars and universals. Such play and oscillation can be seen in the following transcription:

A: The client wants a new can opener, a better one . . .

B: What does better mean?

A: What would an ideal can opener have?

C: Ideally cans shouldn't have to be opened. . . . They should open themselves.

D: Okay, okay. But we're working for a can opener client, not a can company. If you don't like this assignment go sell a new product job to American Can.

E: I hate the way a can opener gets so filthy. . . . Ever looked at the knife part after opening a can of sardines? It smells for days.

A: All right . . . our job must be perfectly clean. What else?

C: Well, if we must stick with the mundane limitations . . . I don't like to think that I have to eat a little steel every time I open up a can.

B: What the hell are you talking about?

C: Listen. When the cutter goes around it removes material. Just be happy that you don't get a big sharp sliver of metal in your tomato soup.

A: Whether present can openers do what you say or not our job better be free of it. What else?

D: It would be great if you could put the top of the can back on . . . you know, for cat food and stuff like that.

A: I'll buy that, but I don't think it's a matter of life and death.

D: How about having the unit automatic? Just put in the can and the top is off.

A: That wouldn't be a basic invention. It would just be putting the thing on wheels.

B: We aren't going to get anywhere if we limit our thinking to improvements. My understanding is that the client wants a radically new can opener . . . not a slightly better one.

A: I think you're right. Let's back way off from the problem. . . . What does "open" mean?

B: To me, "open" means that something was closed . . . now it's open.

C: What about a crater? It's always open, isn't it?

D: Sure . . . but that's not what "open" means to me.

E: Both of you are using "open" to describe a state. I think of it as describing an action . . . I "open" the book. The book was closed, now I open it.

A: I wonder if we can universalize it. If we use the word as a verb, does it always imply a previously closed state? . . . I guess it does at that.

E: In nature . . .

A: What?

E: In nature there are things that are completely closed, then open up . . . a clam for instance.

B: But with a clam the process is reversible. We don't need that for our problem. We don't need to close the can up again.

D: I thought it would be great if we could.

B: All right. But the clam isn't actually sealed. The shell fits nicely together but it's not soldered like a can. The only analogy from nature would have to be a case where something is wounded and heals immediately.

E: If a starfish loses one of his legs he grows another one in its place.

B: True. But that's not an opening, is it?

E: I guess not . . . How about a pea pod? That really opens up along a line . . . it's got a built-in weakness and splits along the weak line.

A: Has a can got a built-in weakness? A weakness we can take advantage of?

C: Maybe it's weak where the top is put on. Around the seams.

D: Hell no! It's stronger there than anywhere else. It's double thickness there on the seam.

B: Maybe it's only apparently stronger there. If you cut along the outside edge at least you wouldn't get the cutter all dirty. . . . And no filings could drop into the food either.

E: (at the blackboard) Let's see. The seam in a can looks like this . . . double where the two layers of metal are rolled over. If we just cut into the first layer and peeled it back. . . .

B: You know that's not bad. If you did that then you'd have a top that could be put back on. It would be larger than the diameter of the can itself.

A: Not only that, but the top couldn't fall back into the can. Wouldn't need magnets the way they have them on the models I've seen. Just pick the top off the can.

By playing with the word "open" the group was able to detach itself from a view too close to present can opener art (note that this play led to the use of Direct Analogy). It was not till the group began to universalize the word "open," however, that they began to become productive. On the other hand, the session would have been a failure if the participants had simply filled a bushel basket with their associations to "open." By constantly comparing their associations with the can opener problem as understood they scanned for the analogy which showed them a valuable viewpoint.

Comparable to play with words and meanings is speculative play with logical systems. Logical systems are by definition self-consistent. Consequently, this sort of play involves upsetting or distorting inner consistency. One classic example of this kind of play is Lobachevsky's invention of non-Euclidean geometry. The inner consistency of the Euclidean system of geometry depends upon certain axioms which can be neither proved nor disproved in terms of the system itself. Since a self-consistent system develops the meanings and relationships already inherent in the given axioms, it does not criticize those axioms. Lobachevsky chose one axiom (that in a given plane only one line could be drawn through a given point parallel to another line) and upset this axiom's familiar definition. Lobachevsky played with the possibility of a number of lines drawn through a given point parallel to a given line in a given plane.[9] On this speculative assumption, this new axiom, he built a new system every bit as consistent within itself as the more traditional Euclidean system. Lobachevsky's invention depended on speculative play with the formal definitions of the word "parallel." From this play, the logical and systematic consequences were developed into the first non-Euclidean geometry.

The new geometry formed in this way seemed at first mere wilful play, irresponsible in fact. The closed system of Euclidean geometry was judged to be true, not only logical in itself, but also descriptive of the nature of the space as experienced. This representative accuracy of Euclidean geometry is "true" of everyday spatial relationships in that it enables us to handle those relationships with "reasonable" accuracy. However, this "representative ac-

[9] *The Encyclopædia Britannica,* 13th edition, Vol. 15, p. 835 and Vol. II, p. 727.

curacy" is a function of traditional ways of perceiving and categorizing our experience of everyday space, traditional ways which are accepted but are neither true nor untrue. Lobachevsky's invention has therefore two important consequences: 1) It questions the degree of "representative accuracy" which was traditionally attributed to the Euclidean system. Thus Lobachevsky's system tended to make the familiar strange. When we live with the familiar system without questioning it, we lose our awareness of the unfounded (even questionable) assumptions which underlie the system and our acceptance of it. We attribute a false concreteness to what in reality is only a symbolic representation, a conceptual tool. When the established system was questioned in a "strange" way by Lobachevsky the system, its assumptions, and its implications became more clear for what it was. 2) Lobachevsky's invention also makes it possible at least to conceive (if not to see) other ways of interpreting the human experience of space. Contemporary concepts of the nature of the nuclear astro-physical world would be impossible if we were still locked into the assumption that Euclidean geometry provides the final symbolic language for the expression of spatial relationships.[10]

Language itself—mathematical symbols or words and phrases—when combined into a logical self-consistent pattern threatens constantly to deceive us as being "concrete," as not only expressing ways of thinking, but also being the way things in themselves are. This threat to constructive imagination assumed two interrelated forms: 1) over-development of expertly elaborated systems of internal consistency; 2) over-development of "apparent" and everyday concreteness. Thus Euclidean geometry, over-developed as a self-consistent system, tends to atrophy in a meaningless closed circle of expertise. Over-developed as concrete and self-evidently valid, it atrophies by becoming confused with a representative description of actual space.

Making the familiar strange and sustaining that strangeness requires a constant vigilance to reawaken the evocative quality of

[10] Bell, E. T., *Men of Mathematics* (New York: Simon and Schuster, 1937), pp. 294–306.

comparison relationships. It involves achieving new ways to ask old questions: Everybody knows what the word "open" means. Only by devising a new way to ask the question: "What does *open* mean?" can we re-project the metaphoric and speculative potential inherent in the universal (open) and in the particulars (examples of *open* and *openness*) which interplay with that universal.

Basically, Synectics' concern with these new ways of asking old questions is not so much with their end results as it is with how the asking can provide the mechanisms necessary to initiate and sustain the process of creation. The immediate goal of play with language and with logical pattern is less "ultimate order" and more the achievement of a coincidence of meaning and excitement which can be accepted as valid and which can simultaneously excite an energetic and work-oriented response.

The sciences and the arts make relevant the apparent irrelevancies which abound in the fantastic multiplicity of human experience. Isaac Newton invented a scientific pattern in which apparent irrelevancies are harmoniously arranged so that the mind coherently can take in the whole without neglecting the details. Picasso's "Guernica" pulls into an esthetic order what would otherwise be a wide range of unrelated and conflicting visual experience. The creative mind in process realizes a higher order of relevance which lends meaning to what we would normally or logically regard as a collection of irrelevant details. Formal processes of logical thought can't achieve this end. "If the quest for a pure objectivity in statement could succeed, it would achieve a pure meaninglessness. A purely objective statement would have to be made by nobody to nobody."[11]

A syllogism is the classic form of this closed circle of relevancy; to be caught in a syllogism is like being trapped in a doorless closet. The syllogism is closed and cold, but it is internally relevant. *X* is *Y; Y* is *Z;* therefore *X* is *Z*. Socrates is a man; all men are mortal; Socrates is mortal. True, obvious, banal; but if we try to

[11] MacMurray, John, "Some Reflections on the Analysis of Language," *Philosophical Quarterly,* vol. I (1951), p. 319–337.

inject another kind of assumption, e.g., Rodin's "Thinker" is a man; all men are mortal; Rodin's "Thinker" is mortal, then something goes wrong. The initial assumption is, on one level, reasonable, but it is external to the syllogism which only guarantees inner relevancy and truth. The syllogism doesn't care whether Rodin's "Thinker" is a man or a statue. Caring (or in this case the ability to see the man in the marble) is outside the province of the syllogism. Logical systems like the syllogism are capable only of egocentric relevance. They cannot admit irrelevancies like "caring" or confusing men with marble; they cannot admit the sense of humor or the imaginative leap which establishes a relationship not already implied by a general proposition.

A special case of the closed circle of logical methodology is the method of "possibility destruction." This method is often assumed to be the new science in which computers, human, mechanical, and electronic, sift through masses of irrelevant data to single out the relevant fact. This method is in practice an extension of logical systematics. It is simply a random and mechanized way of looking for the one needle of truth already implicit in an established logical judgment or hypothesis, and its relation to the haystack of apparently irrelevant data is a purely mechanical one.

Neither logic as a system nor computer-oriented "science" is capable of the reaches of metaphoric and analogic relevance which the creative imagination can develop in its search for forms. The achievement of these higher orders of relevancy, enriched and widely diverse patterns of association, requires a redefinition of that which is traditionally accepted as relevant. The contemporary tendency in all walks of life (including, unfortunately, science and the arts) is to limit areas of relevance in the vain hope that narrow limits will offer a secure life and a simple, readily understandable position in terms of which to work. We are, in effect, taught to order the world of experience by a process of exclusion. We handle the fantastic multiplicity of experience by a combination of rejection and explanation, where the effort to explain is really an effort to settle—to package an observation of—something irrelevant, so that we can be secure by hiding the rich ambiguous data of our surroundings.

THE TOLERATION AND USE OF IRRELEVANCE

To learn the toleration and use of the apparently irrelevant is to learn new techniques of perceiving and ordering experience. These techniques enable the individual to retain his "peripheral vision" and to achieve order by inclusion and through a plasticity of awareness and consciousness. In many ways, this plasticity is characteristic of the child's approach to the world's multiplicity; thus, as in learning how to play, so in learning how to accept and to use the irrelevant, the individual is involved in relearning, on an adult level, techniques which were "natural" in the intuitive vision of childhood. It is axiomatic that the child's vision is dulled as he is schooled to the regimented responses which will be expected and required of him in an adult world. The childlike and intuitive "plasticity of vision" necessary to creativity on an adult level involves a paradox: it is childlike, but it is also the childlike transposed, informed by an adult sense of responsibility and purposiveness. Ironically, the groundwork for this responsibility and purposiveness is laid by the educative process, depressing the child in us and rendering us practical dullards. This paradox in turn implies the necessity for dynamic balance which reawakens childlike plasticity within the context of adult controls. Through the examination of tapes and through individual interviews, Synectics research has identified several different kinds of irrelevance as well as ways for the apparently irrelevant to become meaningful and useful. Irrelevance takes three general forms:

1. irrelevant perceptions, ideas and generalities;

2. irrelevant emotional factors (Hedonic Response: Autonomy of Object);

3. accidents.

IRRELEVANT PERCEPTIONS, IDEAS,
AND GENERALITIES

In the normal course of the day an adult individual is bombarded by a fantastic multiplicity of data which are irrelevant to whatever he happens to be doing. To focus (even momentarily) on all of these data is to flirt with insanity. The nervous system acts as a primary filter but the human individual must extend this editing process in order to prevent a level of distraction which would make any purposive activity impossible. Carrying this editing process to the normal adult extremes prevents distraction but inhibits the kind of learning essential for creative activity.

How can one sustain the dynamic balance between distraction and learning? How does one select the apparent irrelevancy which will trigger the kind of vision that leads to artistic or technical invention? A productive artist, scientist or inventor must chew upon and digest more than a single bit of the universe. He plays with bundles of apparent irrelevancies, hoping to make them coalesce in inventive relevance. But how does he know when he is distracting himself, going too far afield? Insofar as the mind can permit the specific creative problem to oscillate in and out of consciousness, there is practically no observation, perception, idea, or generality which is not potentially useful to a solution. As long as the mind remains tied to the problem at hand, as long as the problem so occupies the foreground of the mind as to prevent any looking beyond it, the positioning of the problem will block the "peripheral vision" which can comprehend and use the apparently irrelevant. It is not a matter of logically tracking down the meaningful irrelevancy, but a matter of preparing the mind for its occurrence.

One inventor whom we observed and questioned at some length provided a clear-cut example of this process. He was faced with the task of inventing a system for heavy army tanks to get over bottomless crevasses up to 10 feet wide. In the early stages of his work, he described his mind as going around and around as though faced with a keyless Chinese puzzle. This stage lasted for nearly three weeks. He was so completely involved in the problem that it had become hallucinatory for him. Quite formally, as if performing a ritual, he got into his car, drove into the country, and took a walk.

He literally sought distraction; through a conscious effort he forced the problem to retreat sufficiently to permit him to take an interest in the irrelevancies which surrounded him. It was autumn and he sat down under a maple tree and detachedly watched the leaves fall in miniature tornadoes. He idly recalled the meteorological generalities that accounted for the pigmy cyclones. He speculated about the process of color change in the maple leaves. The tank-bridging problem slipped into the background of his mind, not forgotten, but off stage, waiting for a cue.

At this point in the process, when the tank-bridge problem was removed from the foreground of his mind, he stopped to watch two ants working their way up the bark of an elm tree. He saw them as two mountain climbers on a rope. As he ambled on, he daydreamed about the ants and their ability to lift weights many times their own. The daydream expanded to include ants lifting each other over obstacles on the tree bark, and then shifted to concentrate on the fantasy of two ants halted by a tiny chasm through which a rivulet was running. The inventor reported a strong sense of immediacy in the succession of daydream images which followed. The ants' feelers flitted about frantically. Finally, one ant got a grip on the edge of the precipice, and the other ant walked far enough out on his brother insect to get a grip on the other side of the chasm. He then pulled himself and his companion up and over.

As the inventor was watching the ants and subsequently entertaining fantasy constructs of his own, the tank-bridge problem was not forgotten but displaced by the focus of his attention on an apparent irrelevancy, first in the natural world and later in his imagination. Then the ants with their armored exoskeletons reminded him of his tanks and the problem was re-evoked into his consciousness. He turned the play experience into a reality response. He compared the analogy implied by his fantasy with his problem. He saw how, by welding special hitches to the front and the rear of each tank, the tanks, like the ants, could be connected to form their own bridge at will. As six tanks came to a crevasse, they would link up; the rear tanks would support the first tank in space until it got a grip on the opposite side. Thus, all the vehicles would be pulled over.

Several different kinds of apparent irrelevancy as well as ways in which an inventor hunts and scans for what is relevant in irrelevance are exemplified in this case. His observations of the small cyclones and the leaves did not turn out to be relevant to the problem now residing in his preconscious. Even his visual observation of the ants was not relevant. In fact, not till he began to daydream and conjure up the fantasy of the two ants crossing the chasm did this combination of irrelevant observations and imaginings make it possible for the inventor to see a new viewpoint for a possible solution. How? He was hunting for a new way of looking at his problem. On the one hand his mind was playing with the pair of ants. On the other hand, his mind was scanning for potential relevance in the details of his insect reverie. Reverie alone would have been mere subjective fantasy. Scanning alone would have been mere possibility destruction. The integration of the two resulted in the viewpoint leading to a solution.

HEDONIC RESPONSE: AN IRRELEVANCE FILTER

Hedonic response as evoked in creative process, takes two forms: 1) it is a pleasurable feeling, developed toward the successful conclusion of a period of problem-solving concentration, that signals the conceptual presence of a major new viewpoint which promises to lead to a useful solution; 2) it is a pleasurable feeling which occurs in a minor way acting as a moment-to-moment evaluation of the course of the creative process itself.

Emotional response is distrusted in science and technical invention. This is because the way one feels about the solution to a problem is confused with emotional response to a problem during the process of searching for a solution. Artists and writers are *expected* to like or dislike their materials and subject matter. The products of art and literature are judged on a "like" or "dislike" basis whereas the criterion of technological products is "are they useful?", "do they work?" Esthetic products are criticized irrationally, subjectively; scientific products are examined rationally, objectively. Synectics accepts this traditional value philosophy but emphasizes that the *process* of producing either esthetic or technical objects is accompanied by certain useful emotional responses, and that these responses must not be rejected as irrelevant, but must be schooled and liberated. Hedonic Response is one of the important responses.

How can one select from the multiplicity of everyday perceptions and speculations those which will enable one to achieve a higher order of coherence? Synectics research has found that selection is always hedonic and essentially esthetic—rarely, if ever, logical. The tank-bridge inventor felt that there was "something right," he felt a Hedonic Response about the viewpoint resulting from his fantasy about two ants crossing the chasm. Synectics uses the technique of "controlled pleasure seeking," of scanning for the human experience of Hedonic Response when selecting this viewpoint rather than the other. While the degree of success in the use of Hedonic Response varies in direct relation to the amount of "practice" an individual or a group has had, the results have been consistently positive, implying that the skills involved in this technique can be learned not so much by precept as by practice and example.[12]

In reviewing the literature remotely and closely connected with creative process the expression "intuition" recurs. How is it that certain creative thinkers continually select avenues of approach, viewpoints which turn out to have elegant solutions? Intuition! How out of the infinity of irrelevant data are those useful elements se-

[12] See "Appendix I—Hedonic Response."

lected which turn out to underlie useful solutions? Intuition! What is intuition and how can it be used in terms of teaching people to increase the chance of success when faced with problem-stating, problem-solving situations?

Hedonic Response is that warm feeling of "being right" long before there is any pragmatic rationale, any examination of the validity of this pleasurable feeling. Those people who, beyond what could be expected from probability alone, select avenues of thought which turn out to be constructive have learned to listen to their intuitive feeling of Hedonic Response. They subconsciously remember that in the past this feeling has in fact led to constructive results. They associate this feeling with success.

Hedonic Response has been tested in Synectics research in this way: in order to have a record of what transpired all sessions were taped. When a breakthrough or a new viewpoint had been made, the tape was reviewed with the person who verbalized the new viewpoint so that he could be questioned about how he felt at the time. Inevitably this person felt that he was "going to be right." Not that he *was* right but that he was *going to be* right. He would describe the warm promise of success over the horizon—not here and now, but glitteringly close. Synectics shows trainees how to be on the lookout for Hedonic Response by having them listen to a taped session. This is followed by discussion of the experience with the man who articulated the breakthrough. Tentatively the student tries to listen to himself. He has seen it "work" in the case of the individual who described the feeling to him and this gives the novice confidence to try to listen to himself. At first he is apprehensive, self-conscious, because this is his irrational self speaking. He must understand that Hedonic Response is making conscious a subconscious element of creative process.

There is considerable evidence of Hedonic Response, this "learned delirium," in the writings of various proved creative people. Dorothy Canfield said about beginning a story: "I get simultaneously a strong thrill of intense feeling . . . I recognize it for the 'right' one when it brings with it an irresistible impulse . . .

when it comes, the story is begun."[13] Poincaré speaks of the "feeling of absolute certitude accompanying the inspiration" but he warns that "often the feeling deceived us without being any less distinct on that account."[14] Synectics theory holds that creative people continually use Hedonic Response and take this rather than the alternative path because they subconsciously remember that in the past the response indicated that they had been on the right track. Synectics is a technique to make this feeling conscious for people who have not learned to "listen" to it. As in the case of the mechanisms it can be learned, and after being learned it drops back into the level of automatic implementation.

Blake said: "You have the same intuition as I, only you do not trust or cultivate it. You can 'see' what I do, if you choose."[15] Edison possessed a remarkable ability to make hypotheses and guesses which, when tested, turned out to be true.[16] He had "learned" to trust the feeling of certainty and pleasure that accompanies Hedonic Response. Sir Joshua Reynolds believed that constructive creative activity was "the result of the accumulated experience of our whole life" and he warned against "an unfounded distrust of the imagination and feeling, in favor of narrow, partial, confined, argumentative theories."[17]

Great artists, philosophers, and scientists at least subconsciously employ the psychological state of Hedonic Response. Einstein's working procedure, for instance, is analogous to that of the artist. "Once he has come upon a problem, his path toward solution is not a matter of slow, painful stages. He has a definite vision of the possible solution, and considers its value and the methods of ap-

[13] Heydick, B. A., ed., *Americans All* (New York: Harcourt, Brace, 1920). "How 'Flint & Steal' Started & Grew" by Dorothy Canfield Fisher.

[14] Poincaré, Henri, *Science and Method,* tr. Francis Maitland (New York: Dover, 1956), p. 56.

[15] Gilchrist, Alexander, *Life of William Blake,* 2 vols. (London: Macmillan, 1880), Vol. 1, p. 364.

[16] Dyer, F. L. and Martin, T. C., *Edison, His Life and Inventions,* 2 vols. (New York: Harper, 1910), Vol. II, p. 620.

[17] Reynolds, Sir Joshua, *Literary Works,* 2 vols. (London: T. Cadell & Wm. Daves, 1797), Vol. 1, pp. 170–172.

proaching it." Einstein, when faced with a problem, had a "definite vision of its solution." In other words, he intuitively thought that the solution would be "so and so" and acted accordingly.[18] Schopenhauer said, "If I faintly perceive an idea which looks like a dim picture before me, I am possessed with an ineffable longing to grasp it. I leave everything and follow my idea through all its tortuous windings, as the huntsman follows the stag."[19] Edison's ability to guess correctly ". . . frequently enabled him to take short cuts to lines of investigation whose outcome verified in a most remarkable degree statements made offhand and without calculation."[20]

The inventor scans or hunts for the feeling which signals elegance and pleasure to him. In Pavlovian style he reacts when the "bell" of elegance rings and he gets that positive hedonic feeling. This feeling is indeed pleasurable. So pleasurable is it that there are many would-be inventors who refuse to go beyond it lest an experiment disprove the principle and withdraw the sanction of the pleasurable feeling. On the other hand, the successful inventor who dares to test the principle underlying his novel concept has the best of both worlds: he has the satisfaction of "feeling" the solution is near, plus the extra pleasure of seeing his feeling justified.

AUTONOMY OF OBJECT

During the creative process Hedonic Response is experienced immediately before, though intimately interconnected with, what Synectics calls Autonomy of Object. The feeling that a certain viewpoint will lead to a solution is prior to even the earliest stages of the concrete solution itself. The first sign of the concrete solu-

---

[18] Reiser, A., *Albert Einstein* (London: Thornton Butterworth Ltd., 1931), pp. 116–117.

[19] Zimmern, H., *Schopenhauer: His Life and Philosophy* (London: George Allen & Unwin Ltd., 1932), p. 45.

[20] Dyer, F. L. and Martin, T. C., *Edison, His Life and Inventions* (New York: Harper, 1910), Vol. 2, p. 620.

tion itself appears when the concept begins to have a life of its own. In the course of making the familiar strange and even during the experience of Hedonic Response, the individual is in control. There is no dualism of subject and object. However, once the vaguest implication of the concrete solution has been articulated, even though not completely understood, it cannot be denied. It survives. It begins to have the capacity to act as an entity separate from the minds who made it. Sometimes it is necessary to review the tape to see clearly the birth, evolution, and survival of a concept which has begun to have autonomy of its own.

In the course of the creative process the individual responsible for the creative activity must permit what has been constructed to live its own life—to lead on. Thackeray once said, "I don't control my characters; I am in their hands and they take me where they please."[21] When Balzac was criticized for producing a hero who went from one tragic contretemps to another he answered, "Don't bother me . . . these people have no backbone. What happens to them is inevitable."[22] Much has been made of the fact that the artist fabricates whereas the scientist discovers. However, these quotations show that the data of the artist in the course of creative process are often as objective and external as those of the technician. Dreiser believed that "where there is no plot there is apt to be literary merit. The reason for the absence of plot in a great novel is that it interferes with the logical working out of the destinies of the characters. The presence of a plot obliges the novelist to make concessions here and there so that the plot will work out to its proper denouement."[23] How like a criticism of invalid science is Dreiser's critique of an overplotted novel! Invalid science exists where the research has been worked out to satisfy a preconceived notion of the scientist rather than to describe the observed facts. In the art of the novel as in science, then, the data must be respected

[21] Melville, Lewis, *William Makepeace Thackeray* (London: Ernest Benn Ltd., 1927), pp. 253–254.

[22] Lawton F., *Balzac* (London: Grant Richards, 1910), p. 92.

[23] Hogarth, Basil, *The Techniques of Novel Writing* (London: John Lane, The Bodley Head Ltd., 1934), p. 51.

as autonomous, as having the virtue of life. In both art and science the phenomena of nature as perceived atomistically are incoherent. The mind of man brings order to the perceived data of the universe. Any invention is a particular example of general order. In an invention experience the early signs of inventive order (problem-solving) constitute the birth of Autonomy of Object.

PURPOSIVENESS

Review of the taped sessions reveals a strong thread of purposiveness leading to inventive solutions. There is a direct relation between the strength and vitality of purpose (the earlier it appears in the session the better, for example) and the soundness and novelty of the solution achieved in a given session. Repeatedly we attempted to feed back this purposiveness into succeeding sessions, but the state was too amorphous to be effective. There appears to be a goal toward which the entire process tends; in fact, the whole unconscious purposefulness of a session is embodied in the state of Autonomy of Object. Although this state is operating all along, it is not clearly manifest until a solution begins to form. Then in retrospect all the preceding effort appears purposeful and somehow directed. At the start of a session there is much amorphous conversation apparently leading nowhere. But when the early glimmer of a solution begins to take command then this glimmer dictates the form of the solution. Because this state is temporally posterior to the main body of the process we have been unable to reduce it to a mechanism.

ACCIDENT AS IRRELEVANCE

Accident is in effect the irrelevant in motion. We call those things which happen unexpectedly, as we move, accidents. Our tendency is to regard them as interrupting our intentions. When an adult intends to carry a pail of water along an established path, if the water spills, his intention has been interrupted; automatically he closes his mind to the effect of the spilled water on a patch of earth or the pattern that has been spattered on the ground. A child's notice lies at the opposite extreme; he is usually willing to accept the interruption, to focus on the chance effects and designs which have resulted. In fact, it is the child's eternal focusing on accidental irrelevancies which pushes adult patience to the breaking point.

One of the most famous examples of the willingness and ability to accept, perceive, and use an accident is Goodyear's discovery of the vulcanizing process. What intended course of action was interrupted when Goodyear dropped the crude rubber on the stove we cannot know. Goodyear could have rejected the accident as irrelevant to his intentions. But he accepted the accident, observed its results, broadened the narrow, preconceived field of what he was doing, and thus achieved the discovery—instead of sweeping the accidentally vulcanized piece of rubber into the trash bin. There were three other people in the room when the "accident" occurred, and they failed to recognize the small piece of vulcanized rubber as having any meaning or importance.[24] It remained for Goodyear not only to perceive, but also to convince others that the result had value. The attitude of mind required for this kind of perception is a willingness to entertain the possibility that any accident, distraction, or interruption may be revealing.

The spilled contents of a garbage pail on a kitchen floor are hardly a "happy accident." Kitchen floors are supposed to be kept clean and a natural response to the spilled garbage is rejection—we mop up the mess that has violated a primary intention (the clean floor). A trained eye capable of temporarily suspending the clean floor prejudice might see in the colors, textures, and patterns of the garbage an interesting moment of design. The attitude of mind which rigidly carries out established intentions precludes learning, except in the nar-

[24] Goodyear, Charles, *Gum Elastic and the Discovery of Vulcanization* (New Haven: Published for the author 1885), Vol. I, pp. 118–119.

rowest of ways, because according to this attitude accidents and all
orders of irrelevance must be rejected as foreign, distracting, and in-
terruptive to accepted codes of importance and relevance.

The tradition of accidental discovery is as strong in our culture
as it was in the past. Souriau, perhaps the first to publish a book dealing solely with the subject, overemphasized the role of chance in
invention.[25] Although Ernst Mach at times seemed to agree with
Souriau, his experience as an inventive scientist made him aware of
certain nonaccidental functions of process which occur in the course
of discovery. "The historian, the philosopher, the jurist, the mathematician, the artist, the aesthetician, all illuminate and unfold their
ideas by producing from the rich treasure of memory similar, but
different, cases; thus, they observe and experiment in their
thoughts."[26] Later Mach describes analogy: "That relationship between systems of ideas in which the dissimilarity of every two homologous concepts as well as the agreement in logical relations of every
two homologous pairs of concepts, is clearly brought to light, is
called an analogy."[27]

Elsewhere Mach says, "Every motive that prompts and stimulates
us to identify and transform our thoughts proceeds from what is new,
uncommon, and not understood."[28] Nowhere does Mach suggest the
possibility of successful discoverers having at least unconsciously
trained themselves to "make" accidents by operating along the lines
implied by his statements; and of course he does not concern himself
with this kind of "training" being implemented at a conscious level.
Yet, Synectics theory is based upon the fact that certain individuals
make creative contributions at a rate greater than could be expected
from probability alone. To attribute the success of these individuals
to accidents is to imply a cosmology that somehow favors them and
not others. Synectics favors Pasteur's dictum, "Dans les champs de

[25] Souriau, Paul, *Theorie de l'Invention* (Paris: Librairie Hachette et Cie.,
1881), pp. 59–69.
[26] Mach, Ernst, *Scientific Lectures,* tr. T. J. McCormack (Chicago: Open
Court Publishing Co., 1895), p. 230.
[27] *Ibid,* p. 250.
[28] *Ibid,* p. 224.

l'observation le hasard ne favorise que les esprits préparés,"[29] but goes even further to say that characteristic of "les esprits préparés" are mechanisms and states which can be understood and implemented.

CONCLUSION

The experience of Hedonic Response is the highest order of excitement. The emotional satisfaction inherent in Hedonic Response is a vital element in the motivation of creative people who, once having known the thrill, are driven to realize it again and again. Since the only way to gratify this impelling desire is to work through the experience of creating basic novelty, those who are so compelled must invent continually; they become addicted to re-evoking Hedonic Response.

Closely allied with the energy-release resulting from the feeling of right direction is the energy released when individual or group achieves a close empathic identification with concept and implement. This achievement of a state of involvement carries with it "a feeling of knowing," a special order of familiarity which is contingent on a real entry into the realm of the strange, discussed before. When the familiar is made strange and involvement with the strange is achieved, the result is the excitement of a high-energy state. The control of this creative energy is implicit in the oscillating motion between involvement and detachment; further it is implicit in the ways by which the search for pleasurable focus is based on testing and probing the validity of the "strange world" about to be entered by means of involvement.

The ability to accept and entertain a wide range of irrelevancy has several interrelated functions in the creative process. It enables the individual to preoccupy and distract his mind and its surfaces at will, as in the case of the tank-bridge inventor, who sought distrac-

[29] "In the field of (scientific) observation chance favors those who are prepared."

tion in order to free preconscious fantasy levels of his mind. This ability to accept irrelevancy implies a willingness to re-examine, at times to reject, established orders.

A rather obvious danger is involved when the irrelevant is pursued as simple distraction, as a means of escape from problems which should be faced, or as a means of prematurely breaking or interrupting concentration. This overdeveloped ability to accept the irrelevant and the accidental leads to psychological dispersion, where the mind drowns. Thus, the use of this ability to accept irrelevancy requires control—the kind of control suggested by the tank-bridge inventor's oscillation between intense and singleminded concentration on the tank-bridge problem and the drifting, open-vision state of mind which characterized his walk in the woods.

The analogies and metaphors resulting from play with the mechanisms define one end of the oscillation spectrum. The other end is defined by the problem as understood. New viewpoint results from the productive integration of the two ends of the spectrum. This new viewpoint is born from "carrying on the very minimum of practical behaviour"[30] on the one hand, and on the other hand, holding firm to the problem as understood.

[30] Tolman, E. C., *Purposive Behavior in Animals and Men* (Berkeley: U. of Cal. Press, 1951), p. 208.

Our culture has seen the rise of the technocrats; witness the increasing activity of scientists in government. These men of special knowledge, of course, contribute to decision making according to their particular abilities in their chosen fields. But the prestige of their knowledge carries over into government as a whole, because the reputation of a man of knowledge is based on technological accomplishments of a non-subjective nature. Once he has proved himself as a technical innovator his distinction as an innovator in general flows over into other areas. He becomes a social force, not just an intellectual power.

This book has emphasized the problem-stating, problem-solving contributions of a Synectics group with respect to the technical aspects of an organization. Only off-hand reference has been made to its potential social contributions. Once a Synectics group has proved itself in the technical area it provides a rationale by which management can view and accept such radical activity in terms of social contributions.

Every mature institution or organization—industrial, governmental or educational—functions according to laws which make up its policy. For example, every company has its own "laws" about personnel, procurement, borrowing money, sales, production, salaries, quality control, customer relations, product line, budgets, advertising, etc. If the laws represent a true response to reality, they will be useful. But often, particularly in the case of an old established company, the laws are habits carried forward from a glittering past. Long-term employees from a middle management level up constitute an intra-organizational community which derives comfort from these familiar laws—obsolete or not. This community is the keeper of the scrolls. The laws are the anthropological shibboleths by which the industrial tribe conducts its ritual of business. A Synectics group is a fifth column acting from within the organization community to make the familiar "laws" strange.

The Synectics mechanisms for making the familiar strange are basic operating elements of creative process in art and science. These mechanisms also are the essential ingredients by which an organization keeps itself vital through building into itself regenerating factors for continued survival. Since a law is the basis for efficient decision making, pushing these "laws" out of phase is a threat to the community which abides by them. At least unconsciously this community resists making the familiar strange. The operation of an in-company Synectics group, as a way of organizing for innovation at all levels, has both a social and technological role. A group as a social force for making the familiar strange is more difficult to deny than an individual. When this group is highly motivated, tightly integrated, trained in productive creative activity and autonomous, then the group will be heard.

Similarly, governments have "laws" covering personnel, defense posture, contracts, foreign policy, public health, etc. These ritual laws of operation are so fixed that they are taken for granted. They are so familiar that their validity is taken as self-evident. Thus, for instance, if the political party in control of congress and the presidency wishes to act progressively, its intentions may be mired by unconscious acceptance of the old laws—the old rituals of action. Synectics techniques may prove a useful tool for overcoming these rituals in the areas of government or industrial policy.

The following transcript is edited from a tape recording of an experimental Synectics session devoted to the government problem of science and public policy. Various mathematical models of the problem had been worked through, but the group decided that the syllogistic inorganic nature of the mathematical model was no place to start—it was agreed that the initial conceptual solution (model) should be dynamic and concrete. The statement of the problem was "How can we know if our own culture, with respect to military defense and economic posture, is valid? Are we ahead or not? Where should we, as a country, put our government money?" This session

was the first of a series in response to this problem and the participants were drawn from industrial and university faculty sources;
a civil engineer, a chemist with considerable background in over-
seas consulting, a geologist turned advertising executive, a physicist,
and a zoologist.

A: . . . Choosing your diet . . . that's what it's like. . . . The
whole situation reminds me of a castaway who hates citrus—he doesn't
ever eat them. He's getting beri-beri but he doesn't know it till it's too
late.

B: You're making an analogy to the government that doesn't know
it's "starving itself" till the roof falls in . . . then it's too late. They bet
on the wrong horse after it was stolen and the barn door was closed—
to massacre three metaphors.

C: You don't even know you're sick . . . that's what scares me.

D: What do you put your dollars in—if you're the government?

C: Unless you have a war you don't know if that citrus fruit was
necessary or not.

E: The battle is the payoff.

B: You don't know till it's too late.

D: How can you know?

A: If I'm an animal—a nocturnal animal—how do I know I'm winning? Should I be confident or scared? How do I measure this?

B: How are you doing?

A: Fine! I steal from the farmer every night . . . and I seem to be
able to dodge the buckshot.

C: You ought to feel good—you've got the thing worked out.

E: But the buckshot's getting closer and I'm getting jumpy. Maybe
tomorrow night I'll get it in my raccoon behind—right in the ass.

A: Maybe I'd hole up in the woods and hide.

D: But pretty soon there's nothing left, and you get hungry. You
range as far as a raccoon can and you've eaten everything in your
territory.

B: One thing you've got—every night you go out to the farmer's chicken pen—and if you manage to get your supper, then each night you know you're ahead.

D: But you have no way of judging how it'll be tomorrow. Maybe the farmer will have set a booby-trap.

A: Every night I have to risk my life to find out where I stand —but this is a damn good way of knowing whether for the nonce I'm living or not.

E: Are you risking your life to eat for your own survival or to save Mrs. Raccoon and the babies?

A: I don't know. I'm a male. I'm looking out for me. I already would have eaten my family if I were really starving.

C: If you're in the woods and you need chicken you've got to go and find one—you're chicken addicted—you're "hooked" by chickens.

B: But you know the farmer's got that gun—sooner or later he'll wear you down or shoot you full of buckshot.

D: I know what I'd do.

B: What?

D: I'd make friends with the kids—become a pet, like a kitten.

E: Then you've given up your freedom.

A: You'd give up your wild animal freedom.

D: But I'd get my chicken and no buckshot.

C: . . . Okay . . . you'd have to be willing to put up with a hell of a lot. Pretty soon you'd be fed leavings from the plates—garbage not chicken.

E: Passive—passive—absolute surrender!

B: What's the farmer thinking?

D: He loves his kid so he lets me hang around. After a while he'll grow kind of fond of me.

E: I can't stand where this analogy is taking us . . . to a concentration camp—only run like an expensive summer hotel. It's a kept raccoon—a kept woman who's sacrificed all her personality and autonomy for security.

B: Okay . . . let's try another one . . . I'm diving off the Florida Keys. I look at a bunch of fish—big and small. They're all living together for days, happy as kings. Then suddenly a big fish gulps down the nearest little fish—why?

D: Does the little fish give off an attractive odor? Or does the big fish suddenly think, "My God—it's Friday"?

C: You'd think if I'm a little fish and you're a little fish and I see a big fish turn on you and eat you up . . . you'd think I wouldn't hang around there, wouldn't you?

A: Would you know it if you saw it?

C: Can't I put two and two together?

A: Can you? I don't know if a fish can.

B: Little fish don't run till a big fish starts after them . . . they always hope for the best.

D: There must be a signal after a certain number of little fish are gone.

E: If I'm a little fish and a big one gobbles up my brother, I'm not alerted. I figure it's an accident. Eat six of my brothers and I get the picture. I pack my traps and slope for Texas.

B: What does this tell us about science and public policy?

D: How do we know whether we're ahead or not? If not, where should we put our money?

E: We're looking for a diagnostic tool to tell us.

C: . . . Let's take a crack at an industrial model for a minute.

A: What kind?

C: There's no state of cold war more savage than the garment industry.

A: Okay.

C: . . . There's Max and Sam. They hardly talk to each other, and when they do, they lie. . . . "How's business?" . . . "Terrible." "What are your new models like?" "Awful. My best designer just died."

D: Except every year Sam puts on a great style show—wonderful dresses! And he really sinks Max. Max has no design sense, so Max says to himself, "I better send my nephew Louie to spy on Sam—then I'll set up so perfect a production line that I can always catch up and pass Sam.

B: How?

D: Well, Max knows Sam will always have the best styles so he says to himself, "To hell with trying to develop better styles—let Sam spend money on fashion designers—let Sam waste money developing 50 dresses hoping a couple will be successful . . . I'll have Louie tell me which ones are going. Then, with my production facilities and since I've not had Sam's expense of the fancy style shows and the high salary designers I can produce Sam's successful models faster and cheaper than Sam. I know Sam's designers are brilliant. I can't beat Sam any other way."

E: What is Max risking here?

A: Time lag.

E: What?

A: Time lag. Sam gets in fast—gets a reputation—the best outlets. He keeps Max on the defensive.

E: Are you sure? If you're Macy's whom will you buy from, Sam or Max? After all, Max will have the same styles and his productive capacity and low overhead will let him manufacture more economically.

B: Sam is doing a buckshot market test—and Max is using Louie to spy, to pinpoint.

C: There are no patents in this business—no protection.

D: Given the same production facility, then Sam wins.

C: Right. Then Sam will have everything . . . designs and production know-how.

B: But what if only Max is the real production man? If Max is *the* production man—then in which company would you invest?

E: Is Max's nephew Louie the spy in the picture?

B: Sure!

E: Then my dough goes on Max.

B: But what about the time lag?

E: Sam, in order to get a couple of winners, must disproportionately tie up his capital. He'll never reach Max's production.

A: Max is a parasite—particularly with Louie the spy. He steals—he doesn't create.

D: Then if Sam dies—Max dies—right?

A: Not if Sam is his only competitor, because then Max sells last year's models.

C: Let's drag Louie back in. If we superimpose and compare the Louie analogy with the science and public policy problem we would be apt to decide to decrease the national defense budget and put the extra dough into our spy system.

B: Is there any chance of Sam making a design breakthrough . . . a bias cut that only his cutter knows how to make?

E: Maybe.

C: Sam could be cuter than that. If he knows Max has just made a big investment in a certain kind of production tool, then Sam should come out with designs which can't be adapted to Max's brand new costly machines. Then he's really screwed Max.

B: Sure. Max finds a good buy in a button hole machine. Buys 100 of them. It's no secret. Sam knows, so he makes certain that *all* his new models don't have any buttons.

C: It seems to me that Louie is the critical guy here. . . . In other words, better yet we put our money in the C.I.A. and to hell with the rest.

D: How come? Sam knows what women will like—want to buy.

C: He's employed some talented homosexuals who hate women and therefore design hideous things for them to wear.

B: I'm interested in Sam's designs making some kind of a breakthrough that Max simply can't follow.

A: Where, as an investor will you put your money—with Max or Sam?

E: If I need to live off the income now—I'll go with Max. But if I can afford to risk and wait I'll bet on Sam in the hope that Sam will *really* hit a style breakthrough and I'll clean up.

A: If you don't need any income now because you're eating—but you somehow know you'll need a bundle in five years or you'll go to jail, then you have to go with Sam. No regular income will do you any good. You need the big payoff.

E: Maybe we have to go with Louie but I'd like to hedge my bet . . .

B: Hey! The question is what would you do if you could only go with one—Max *or* Sam?

E: Hell! If Louie's smart I'm with Max. Then I'll have everything—all Sam's ideas plus Max's production capacity.

D: I've got a worry. What good is Louie in this business?

E: What?

A: Look—in the garment business a fellow like Max has got to know which of Sam's models are winners as soon as Sam knows. There's no lag time. If you wait to see which of Sam's models are ordered, by the time they're on the racks in the stores and going like hot cakes and Max knows they're the ones to copy—it's too late. By that time Sam's working on next year's models, having taken the cream of the market.

E: Now wait a minute! Louie would know which models the buyers liked. It's the buyers who are critical here. They are the barometers.

C: If Louie is there, Max is in!

A: Yes—except the buyers select 20 models of which only 5 will be real winners.

C: Then what good is Louie?

A: My feeling now is that I'd go with Sam—he'll always be ahead of Max—and I don't see Max catching up.

E: You've just fired Allen Dulles. That's against the law.

D: If you have a very short time lag I don't see that Louie—or the C.I.A. is any good.

B: Particularly if Sam makes a real breakthrough.

E: Let's say we don't spend a penny on Louie-type C.I.A. Do we put the money we save in the bank?

B: In the Max-Sam situation I'd invest in Sam. I'd put my money on him on the condition that he would attempt to increase the probability of breakthrough.

E: If Sam knew how to do that he'd be doing it, wouldn't he?

B: My feeling is that Sam doesn't reach way out. He's excellent at judging style acceptability year by year, but no good at pulling off the wild play.

C: Let me see if I get you. Re science and public policy you're saying, "Put the Louie money on nonconformist approaches."

D: I rather like that.

C: Me too. . . . The typical Sam approach tends to be based on a restricted imagination level. What I mean is that the very fact that his dress designers are experts may dictate against bringing in a way-out winner.

A: Right. And I don't see Sam, unless pushed, being unconventional in selecting design talent—he's in business and hesitates to hire someone without experience.

C: I'm reminded of the absurd basis for deciding on who should get the government research contracts. The company with the largest list of experts wins.

E: After all—the government has to have some basis for evaluating competence.

D: Careful. You're going against the law of competence.

C: Competence! My barber I want to be competent. My research people I want to be brilliant.

The result of this session was the tentative decision that the Counter Intelligence Agency cannot save the United States from having to increase radically its imaginative productive output. I do not say that this conclusion is distinctively novel—or perhaps even correct; the session was experimental. However, the use of the mechanisms of direct, symbolic, fantasy and personal analogies do appear to be efficient tools for breaking through quickly into a potentially useful viewpoint—a viewpoint which, in turn, admits to an operational mathematical model.

My purpose in straying, in the above transcript, from the industrial model is to offer a concrete example of Synectics functioning in other than a product-oriented situation. Synectics research continues to take the form of experimenting with the use of the operational mechanisms as tools in government, education, and in the arts. Of course, the work with industry still constitutes the most important laboratory, but even here the major characteristic is "experimentation."

To date Synectics research has shown that it is possible to teach at least certain people to adopt certain thinking habits which will increase the probability of success in problem-stating, problem-solving situations. Also it appears reasonable to expect that people with "Synectics potential" can be identified. Further, it seems that once these thinking habits are learned they are never totally forgotten. These habits may grow hazy in the course of automatic, as opposed to conscious, employment, but they can be brought back clearly and distinctly through the formal use of the operational mechanisms at a conscious level.

As Synectics research goes on it is expected to reveal further insights. In fact, some of the concepts described in this book may become obsolete. As I said in the first chapter, this book is a report of research in progress.

The meaning of the Synectics expression Hedonic Response has roots in the works of many thinkers of the past. Pythagoras felt he had discovered the secret of the universe in the notion of number.[1] For him the processes of creating and of abstracting were one. His notions matured into a form of mysticism built on abstraction, both in number and in the meaning of words. The modern aesthetic motivation when faced with two notions of equal instrumental value has its source in the Pythagorean reverence for form, for simple whole numbers, in Pythagoras' intoxication with the music of the spheres. Deriving from this notion of "economy" is the concept of pleasure in the elegance of solutions to such problems. This notion of "elegance" is connected to the Synectics view of a goal being preceded by pleasurable mental excitement.

The sudden perception of economy and elegance of solution to an artistic or technical problem is an intuition—an inspiration. According to Plato, (in the *Phaedrus*) an inspiration is an actual breathing of an insight into the mind of man from the mind of "God"—i.e., divine inspiration. Since this implies a kind of madness, Plato's Socrates deplores activity dependent on this "unhealthy" source. Plato preferred sweet reasonableness that can be reduced to formal abstraction. Like Pythagoras, Plato revered the kind of coherence for the universe that is implied by the intercomprehension of number. The ultimate intercomprehension for him was reason. Insights inspirationally derived pushed ambiguity beyond his tolerance and threatened him with universal anarchy. It is not my purpose to criticize Plato's position but only to point out that even the kind of reason which he loved, when continually applied to the phenomenal world, must rely on inspiration beyond reason for its insemination. Through Aristotle and Plotinus, Plato's notions were carried into the middle ages where the concept of inspiration metamorphosed into the concept of revelation. In turn, revelation became intuition in the 19th century. For Benedetto Croce, expression in art is simply intuition, which is a type of knowledge. Since intuition is the only form of art, then the form is not rationally predetermined, but determined by the nature of the process of creation.

[1] Burnet, John, *Early Greek Philosophy* (London: Adams & Charles Black, 1882, 1948), p. 107.

Croce equates intuition with expression. "He who separates intuition from expression never succeeds in reuniting them."[2]

For both Croce and Bergson[3] intuition is the *sine qua non* of creative process, though less so for Bergson.[4] But how can we define intuition operationally? This is the task Synectics sets itself and for which it attempts to construct mechanisms. As the artist depends on intuition for his insights so does the scientist. Intuition is an inner judgment made by the individual about a concept relative to a problem on which he is working. He judges the concept critically and either implements it or does not. The individual with good intuition is the one who, beyond what could be expected from mere probability alone, repeatedly selects the viewpoint which turns out to lead, for instance, to a great painting or an important invention. Synectics theory holds that there is an excitement and feeling of pleasure accompanying the selection of and signalling a valid intuition, and that people can be taught to watch for this feeling of excitement within them. Creative persons have learned to do this subconsciously and Synectics has shown that it can be consciously noted and learned.

In criticizing the idealist's position that the creative process consists of pure intuition, Bosanquet emphasized the role of the external medium, the paints and canvas which the artist uses, the chemicals and symbols which the chemist uses. Shapes suggested to an artist working in wrought iron are different from the shapes suggested to an artist working in clay. Bosanquet aims at showing the impossibility of separating the creative from the contemplative process by stressing the material nature of art, and the preservation of its various media.[5] Where the creative process is pure technique for Croce, Bosanquet disagrees with such thoroughgoing idealism and insists on returning a material "body" to the idealist "soul" for the purpose of maintaining a balanced view of artistic creation. Synectics agrees with Bosanquet's theory of the dualism in creative process, i.e., painter and canvas or chemist and chemicals. The Synectics psychological state of Autonomy of Object (See p. 138) is the early stage of making Bosanquet's insight operational, but for Bosanquet to name this process "intuition" leads

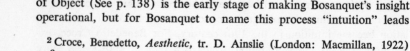

[2] Croce, Benedetto, *Aesthetic*, tr. D. Ainslie (London: Macmillan, 1922) p. 8.

[3] Bergson, Henri, *Creative Evolution*, ed. A. Miller (New York: Henry Holt, 1911).

[4] *Ibid*, p. 177.

[5] Bosanquet, Bernard, *A History of Aesthetic* (London: George Allen and Unwin Ltd., 1892), pp. 444–63.

APPENDICES

157

away from the Synectics purpose of developing operational mechanisms.

Idealist estheticians of intuition and technique, because they assume a continuity of spirit underlying the creative process, do not look for a human desire for increasingly coherent novelty. They feel that a need for beauty is sufficient to motivate creativity, and that the beauty is inherent in the thing described or in the manner of its description. Bosanquet speaks of inherent quality or spirit in the medium. But after stating that creation and contemplation are inseparable, he abandons the problem of how to get feeling into object. He emphasizes the "creative discovery of the right word" rather than the creation of the emotional context. Croce, Bergson, and Bosanquet point out factors which cannot be omitted from even the most generalized description of the creative process, although they are speaking in terms of psychological abstractions rather than concrete experimental psychological states.

APPENDIX II

The following outline of the Synectics process is the basis for putting into practice the various phases of Synectics theory:

Phase 1:   Problem as Given

Phase 2:   Making the Strange Familiar

Phase 3:   Problem as Understood

Phase 4:   Operational Mechanisms

Phase 5:   The Familiar Made Strange

Phase 6:   Psychological States

Phase 7:   States Integrated with Problem

Phase 8:   Viewpoint

Phase 9:   Solution or Research Target.

Problem as Given: For the sake of clarity and simplicity we will assume that the problem is given. The process in the instance where a problem must first be developed is much the same, except that it is longer and somewhat more complicated. The problem as given is the statement of the problem to those responsible for its solution. The statement may turn out to be an accurate description of the state of affairs or it may hide and confuse the basic question. It always implies a labyrinth of interconnected assumptions which may or may not be correct. In the roof example the problem as given was to invent a new roof.

Making the Strange Familiar: Any problem, no matter how old a chestnut, is strange in the sense that concentrated analysis will uncover elements not previously revealed. In this phase it is not important to resolve contrary elements so much as to bring them out into the open. In the roof example making the strange familiar took the form of analysis which revealed the functions as well as the drawbacks of traditional roofs.

Problem as Understood: Profound and determined analysis leads to this phase where the various atomistic bits of information about a problem are isolated for examination. This phase concludes the digestion of the problem as given. In the roof example, the problem as understood was to invent a roof that would change from white to black and vice versa depending on ambient heat and sunlight.

Operational Mechanisms: Analogies (metaphors) are developed which are relative to (and evoked by) the problem as understood. This phase pushes and pulls the problem as understood out of its rigid form of impregnable regularity into a form that offers some conceptual finger-holds. These finger-holds open up the problem as understood. In the roof example the actual mechanism was Direct Analogy—the flounder. However, in a typical Synectics session the mechanisms are interrelated, one leading to another.

The Familiar Made Strange: In this phase the mechanisms have done their job and the problem as understood is seen as foreign. It takes on an interesting cast as though never seen before. In the roof example the analogy of the flounder forced the group to consider a roof in a strange new way—as though it were a flounder's back.

Psychological States: At last the mind's attitude toward the problem as understood attains the states of involvement, detachment, defer-ment, speculation, and commonplace-ness which Synectics theory be-lieves describes the psychological climate most conducive to creative activity. In the roof example the particular states brought into being by the mechanisms were involvement (with the flounder) and deferment from the immediate, from the familiar roof as known, and from solu-tion too soon. (See Ch. II, Conclusions)

States Integrated with Problem: Once the states have been reached through the mechanisms, the most pertinent analogy is conceptually compared with the problem as understood. In this phase the problem as understood is liberated from its old rigid form.

Viewpoint: Looking at a roof as though it were a flounder's back and being able to develop a technical insight into a roof which would solve the problem as understood—this describes the viewpoint phase con-cretely. Each time that analogies derived from the use of mechanisms are compared with the problem as understood a new viewpoint is po-tential, though not necessarily actual. When the comparison is effective in leading to a technical insight into the problem as understood, then the viewpoint is actual. In the roof example the viewpoint resulting from seeing the roof as a flounder's back did in fact lead to a technical insight about how a roof could be made to change from white to black at the proper intervals.

Solution or Research Target: In this phase the viewpoint is reduced to practice in terms of testing the underlying principle, or the viewpoint may become the subject of further research. The activity in this phase depends on whether the viewpoint implies the mere reintegration of known materials in a new way or whether new materials have to be developed.

BIBLIOGRAPHY

ADAMS, Henry, *The Education of Henry Adams*. New York: The Book League of America, 1928.

AGASSIZ, Louis, *Louis Agassiz*. Boston: Houghton Mifflin, 1885.

ALDINGTON, Richard, *The Religion of Beauty*. London: William Heineman Ltd., 1950.

ANDERSON, Maxwell, Carpenter, Rhys, Harris, Roy, *The Bases of Artistic Creating*. New Brunswick: Rutgers University Press, 1942.

ANDREE, S. A., *Andree's Story—Record of Polar Flight*. New York: The Viking Press, 1930.

ANNALS of the New York Academy of Science, *Techniques for the Study of Behavioral Effects of Drugs,* Vol. 65. New York: Academy of Sciences, November 2, 1956.

ARISTOTLE, *Basic Works*. New York: Random House, 1941.

ARMITAGE, Angus, *The World of Copernicus*. New York: New American Library, 1947.

ARNOLD, Thurman W., *The Folklore of Capitalism*. New Haven: Yale University Press, 1937.

BAITSELL, George A. (editor), *Science in Progress*. New Haven: Yale University Press, 1937.

BALDWIN, George B., *The Invention of the Modern Safety Razor: A Case Study of Industrial Innovation*. Cambridge: M.I.T. Pub. in Soc. Science, Series 3, No. 11, 1951.

BALDWIN, James Mark (editor), *Dictionary of Philosophy and Psychology*. New York: Macmillan, 1901.

BARFIELD, Owen, *Poetic Diction*. London: Faber & Faber, 1928.

BARFIELD, Owen, *History in English Words*. London: Methuen & Co. Ltd., 1926.

BAUDOUIN, Charles, *Psychoanalysis and Aesthetics*. London: Allen & Unwin Ltd., 1924.

BAUDOUIN, Charles, *Studies in Psychoanalysis*. London: Dodd, Mead, 1922.

BAUDOUIN, Charles, *Suggestion and Autosuggestion*. London: Dodd, Mead, 1921.

BAUMGARDT, Carola, *Johannes Kepler, Life and Letters*. London: Victor Gollancz Ltd., 1952.

BAXTER, James Phinney, III, *Scientists Against Time*. Boston: Little, Brown, 1946.

BEATTY, Charles, *DeLesseps of Suez*. New York: Harper & Brothers, 1956.

BEAUMONT, Henry and Freeman, Glenn M., *Psychological Factors in Education*. New York: McGraw-Hill, 1949.

BEECHER, Henry K., *Measurement of Subjective Responses: Quantitative Effects of Drugs*. New York: Oxford University Press, 1959.

BELL, E. T., *Men of Mathematics*. New York: Dover Publications, 1937.

BEMIS, Albert Farwell and Burchard, John, II, *The Evolving House: A History of the Home.* Cambridge, Mass.: The Technology Press, M.I.T., 1933, 1936.

BENEDICT, Ruth, *Patterns of Culture: An Analysis of Our Social Structure as Related to Primitive Civilizations.* New York: Penguin Books, 1934.

BENEDICT, Ruth and Weltfish, Gene, *The Races of Mankind.* New York: Public Affairs Pamphlet #85, 1946.

BENNIS, Warren G., *Some Barriers to Teamwork in Social Research.* Cambridge: M.I.T., Department of Economics & Social Sciences, Ser. 2, #54, 1956.

BENNIS, Warren G., *The Social Scientist as Research Entrepreneur: A Case Study.* Cambridge: M.I.T., Department of Economics & Social Sciences, 1955.

BENTLEY, Eric, *The Playright as Thinker.* New York: Noonday Press, 1946.

BERENSON, Bernard. *Aesthetics and History.* New York: Doubleday, 1954.

BERGSON, Henri, *Creative Evolution.* New York: Henry Holt, 1911.

BERKELEY, George, *The Principles of Human Knowledge.* Illinois: Open Court Publishing, 1940.

BIELSCHOWSKY, Albert, *Life of Geothe,* (tr. W. A. Cooper) 3 vols. New York: G. P. Putnam's Sons, 1905.

BIRKHOFF, George D., *Aesthetic Measure.* Cambridge: Harvard University Press, 1933.

BITTER, Francis, *Magnets—The Education of a Physicist.* Garden City, New York: Doubleday Anchor Books, Doubleday & Co., 1959.

BLIVEN, Bruce, Jr., *The Wonderful Writing Machine.* New York: Random House, 1954.

BLOOMFIELD, Leonard, *Linguistic Aspects of Science.* Chicago: University of Chicago Press, 1939.

BOAS, Franz, *Primitive Art.* New York: Dover Publications Inc., 1955.

BOAS, Franz, *Anthropology and Modern Life.* New York: W. W. Norton, 1928.

BOGARDUS, Emory S., *The Making of Public Opinion.* New York: Association Press, 1951.

BOLITHO, William, *Twelve Against the Gods.* New York: Simon & Schuster, 1929.

BONNER, J. T., *Morphogenesis: An Essay on Development.* Princeton: Princeton University Press, 1952.

BOSANQUET, Bernard, *A History of the Aesthetic.* London: Swan Sonnenschein & Co., 1892.

BOSWELL, James, *Boswell's Life of Johnson* (6 vols.). London: Archibald Constable & Co., 1896.

BOYD, T. A., *Charles Franklin Kettering.* New York: E. P. Dutton, 1957.

BOYD, William C., *Genetics and the Races of Man.* Boston: Little, Brown, 1950.

BRIDGMAN, P. W., *The Logic of Modern Physics.* New York: Macmillan, 1946.

BRIFFAULT, Robert and Malinowski, Bronislaw, *Marriage: Past and Present.* Boston: Porter Sargent, 1957.

BRILL, A. A., *Fundamental Conceptions of Psychoanalysis.* New York: Harcourt, Brace, 1921.

BROAD, C. D., *Scientific Thought.* New York: Harcourt, Brace, 1923.

BRONOWSKI, J., *The Common Sense of Science.* Cambridge: Harvard University Press, 1953.

BROOKS, Van Wyck, *John Sloan, A Painter's Life.* New York: E. P. Dutton, 1955.

BULLOUGH, Edward, "Psychical Distance as a Factor in Art and Aesthetic Principle." *British Journal of Psychology,* 1912–13.

BURNET, John, *Early Greek Philosophy.* London: Adam & Charles Black, 1948.

BURTT, E. A., (editor), *The English Philosophers from Bacon to Mill.* New York: Random House, 1939.

CAMPBELL, L., and M. Garret, *The Life of James Clerk Maxwell.* London: Macmillan, 1882.

CARRITT, E. F., *An Introduction to Aesthetics.* London: Hutchinson's University Library, 1949.

CHANDLER, Albert R., *A Bibliography of Experimental Aesthetics 1865–1932.* Columbus, Ohio: Ohio State University, 1933.

CHAPLIN, F. Stuart, *Experimental Designs in Sociological Research.* New York: Harper & Brothers, 1955.

CHRISTIAN, Edgar, *Unflinching: A Diary of Tragic Adventure.* London: John Murray, 1937.

CLIFFORD, William, *The Common Sense of the Exact Sciences.* New York: Alfred A. Knopf, 1946.

COHEN, I. Bernard, *Some Early Tools of American Science.* Cambridge: Harvard University Press, 1950.

COHEN, Morris R., *The Meaning of Human History.* Illinois: Open Court Publishing Co., 1947.

COLLINGWOOD, W. G., *Life of John Ruskin* (2 vols.). Boston: Houghton Mifflin and Company, 1893.

COMPTON, Arthur H., *The Human Meaning of Science.* Chapel Hill: University of North Carolina Press, 1940.

COOKE, E. T., and Wedderburn, Alexander (editor), *The Works of John Ruskin* (2 vols.). New York: Macmillan, 1911.

COUGHLIN, Robert, *Maurice Utrillo.* New York: Harper & Brothers, 1950.

COULSON, Thomas, *Joseph Henry—Life and Work.* Princeton: Princeton University Press, 1950.

CRAFTS, L. W., Scheneirla, T. C., Robinson, E. E., Gilbert, R. W., *Recent Experiments in Psychology.* New York: McGraw-Hill, 1938.

CROCE, Benedetto, *Aesthetic: As Science of Expression and General Linguistic.* London: Macmillan, 1922.

CROWTHER, J. A., *Michael Faraday.* New York: Macmillan, 1920.

CUSS, T. P. Camerer, *The Story of Watches.* Great Britain: Beric Press, 1952.

D'ABRO, A., *The Rise of the New Physics*. New York: Dover Publications, 1939.

DAMPIER, Sir William Cecil, *A History of Science & Its Relations with Philosophy and Religion*. Fourth edition: Revised and Enlarged. Cambridge: Cambridge University Press, 1958.

DANZ, Louis, *Dynamic Dissonance in Nature and the Arts*. New York: Hallmark-Nubner Press, 1952.

DARWIN, Charles, *The Origin of the Species,* Vol. 1 and 2. New York: D. Appleton & Co., 1896.

DARWIN, Charles, *Journal of Researches into the Natural History and Geology of the Countries Visited During the Voyage of H.M.S. Beagle Round the World*. New York: D. Appleton & Co., 1896.

DARWIN, Charles, *The Expression of the Emotions in Man and Animals*. New York: D. Appleton & Co., 1955.

DARWIN, Francis (editor), *Charles Darwin, Life and Letters*. New York: D. Appleton & Co., 1896.

DAVENPORT, Marcia, *Mozart*. New York: Scribner's Sons, 1932.

DESCARTES, Rene, *The Meditations and Selections from the Principles of the Author*. Illinois: Open Court Publishing Co., 1945.

DE TOCQUEVILLE, Alexis, *Democracy in America*. New York: Colonial Press, 1899.

DEWEY, John, *How We Think*. Boston: D. C. Heath, 1910.

DEWEY, John, *Democracy and Education: An Introduction into the Philosophy of Education*. New York: Macmillan, 1924.

DEWEY, John, *Human Nature and Conduct*. New York: Henry Holt, 1922.

DEWEY, John, *The Quest for Certainty: A Study of the Relation of Knowledge and Action*. New York: Minton Balch & Co., 1929.

DEWEY, John, *Problems of Men*. New York: Philosophical Library, 1946.

DOUGLAS, Paul H., *Ethics in Government*. Cambridge: Harvard University Press, 1952.

DRACHMAN, Julian M., *Studies in the Literature of Natural Science*. New York: Macmillan, 1930.

DUTTON, William S., *DuPont: One Hundred and Forty Years*. New York: Scribner's Sons, 1942.

DYER, F. L. and Martin, T. C., *Edison, His Life and Inventions* (2 vols.). New York: Harper & Brothers, 1910.

ECKSTEIN, Gustav, *Noguchi*. New York: Harper & Brothers, 1931.

EDDINGTON, Arthur Stanley, *Science and the Unseen World*. New York: Macmillan, 1929.

EDMAN, Irwin, *Arts and the Man*. New York: W. W. Norton, 1928, 1939.

EINSTEIN, Albert, *Essays in Science*. New York: Philosophical Library, 1933.

EINSTEIN, Albert, *The World as I See It*. New York: Philosophical Library, 1949.

EINSTEIN, Albert, *Relativity*. New York: Henry Holt, 1921.

EINSTEIN, Albert, *Relativity: The Special and General Theory*. New York: Hartsdale House, 1947.

EINSTEIN, Alfred, *A Short History of Music*. New York: Knopf, 1937.

EMERSON, Ralph Waldo, *The Natural History of Intellect*. Boston: Riverside Press, 1893.

EMMET, William LeRoy, *The Autobiography of an Engineer*. Albany, N.Y.: Fort Orange Press, 1931.

EPICURUS, Epictetus, Lucretius, Marc Aurelius, *The Stoic and Epicurean Philosophers*. New York: Random House, 1940.

ERNST and Carrington, *Houdini and Conan Doyle: The Story of a Strange Friendship*. New York: Albert & Charles Boni Inc., 1932.

FARRINGTON, Benjamin, *Francis Bacon: Philosopher of Industrial Science*. New York: Henry Schuman, 1949.

FARRINGTON, Benjamin, *Greek Science II: Theophrastus to Galen*. London: Penguin Books, 1949.

FEARING, Franklin, *Reflex Action: A Study in the History of Physiological Psychology*. Baltimore: Williams & Wilkins Co., 1930.

FLEMMING, Sir Ambrose, *Memoirs of a Scientific Life*. London: Marshall, Morgan & Scott, Ltd., 1934.

FOLLET, M. P., *Creative Experience*. New York: Peter Smith, 1924.

FOULKES, S. H. and Anthony, E. J., *Group Psychotherapy: The Psychoanalytic Approach*. New York: Penguin Books, 1957.

FRANK, Phillip, *Albert Einstein*. New York: Alfred A. Knopf, 1947.

FRANK, Phillip, *Foundations of Physics*. Chicago: Chicago University Press, 1946.

FRANKFORT, Henri, Frankfort, Mrs. Henri, Wilson, John A. and Jacobsen, Thorkild, *Before Philosophy: A Study of the Primitive Beliefs, Myths and Speculations of Egypt and Mesopotamia*. London: Penguin Books, 1949.

FRANKLIN, Benjamin, *Benjamin Franklin*. New York: Pocket Books, Inc., 1938.

FRAZER, Sir James George, *The Golden Bough: A Study in Magic and Religion*. New York: The Book League of America, 1928.

FREUCHEN, Peter, *Arctic Adventure*. New York: Farrar & Rinehart, 1935.

FREUD, Sigmund, *A General Introduction to Psychoanalysis*. New York: Perma Books, 1930.

FREUD, Sigmund, *Moses and Monotheism*. New York: Vintage Books, 1939.

FREUD, Sigmund, *Wit and Its Relation to the Unconscious*. London: Kegan Paul, Trench and Trudner & Co., 1909.

FREUD, Sigmund, *The Origin of Psychoanalysis: Letters to Wilhelm Fliess, Drafts and Notes: 1887–1902*. New York: Basic Books, 1954.

GADE, John A., *The Life and Times of Tycho Brahe*. Princeton: Princeton University Press, 1946.

GALTON, Francis, *Inquiries into Human Faculty and Its Development*. London: J. M. Dent & Sons, Ltd., 1919.

GALTON, Francis, *Hereditary Genius: An Inquiry into Its Laws and Conse-quences.* London: Macmillan, 1892.

GALTON, Francis, *Inquiries into the Human Faculty and Its Development.* London: J. M. Dent & Sons, Ltd., 1919.

GALTON, Sir James, "Thought Without Words," *Nature.* May 1887.

GAMOW, George, *One, Two, Three—Infinity.* New York: The Viking Press, 1947.

GESELL, Arnold, et al., *The First Five Years of Life.* New York: Harper & Brothers, 1940.

GILBERT, Frank, *Jethro Wood, Inventor of the Modern Plow.* Chicago: Rhodes & McClure, 1882.

GOODYEAR, Charles, *Gum Elastic and the Discovery of Vulcanization.* New Haven: published for the author, 1885.

GORDON, William J. J., "Operational Approach to Creativity," *Harvard Business Review.* Vol. 34, No. 6. Nov.–Dec. 1956.

GREGORY, Sir Richard, *British Scientists,* London: Wm. Collins of London, 1941.

GRENFELL, Russell, *Nelson the Sailor.* New York: Macmillan, 1950.

GRIFFIN, Donald R., *Listening in the Dark: The Acoustic Orientation of Bats and Men.* New Haven: Yale University Press, 1958.

GRIGGSON, Geoffrey and Gibbs-Smith, Charles Harvard, *Things: A Volume of Objects Devised by Man's Genius Which Are the Measure of His Civilization.* New York: Hawthorn Books, Inc., 1946.

GRINKER, R. R. and Spiegel, Major John, *War Neuroses.* Philadelphia: Blakiston Co., 1945.

GROOS, Karl, *The Play of Animals* (tr. Elizabeth Baldwin). New York: Appleton-Century, 1898.

GILCHRIST, Alexander, *Life of William Blake* (2 vols.). London: Macmillan, 1880.

HADAMARD, Jacques, *The Psychology of Invention in the Mathematical Field.* Princeton: Princeton University Press, 1954.

HALDANE, J. B. S., *What Is Life?* New York: Boni & Gaer, 1947.

HALL, Anna Gertrude, *Nansen.* New York: Viking Press, 1940.

HAMILTON, Edith, *The Greek Way to Western Civilization.* New York: A Mentor Book, The New American Library, 1948.

HAMILTON, Edith, *Mythology: Timeless Tales of Gods and Heroes.* Boston: Little, Brown, 1942.

HANSON, N. R., *Patterns of Discovery.* Cambridge, England: University Press, 1958.

HARDING, Rosamond, *An Anatomy of Inspiration.* W. Heffer & Sons Ltd., 1940.

HARRIS, Henry, M.D., *The Group Approach to Leadership-Testing.* London: Routledge & Kegan Paul, 1949.

HARVARD GRADUATE SCHOOL of Business Administration, Manufacturing Course, Class of 1955. *Imagination: Undeveloped Resource,* 1955.

HASKINS, Homer, *Studies in the History of Mediaeval Science*. Cambridge: Harvard University Press, 1924.

HATFIELD, H. Stafford, *The Inventor and His World*. New York: Penguin Books, 1933.

HAVENS, Raymond D., *The Mind of a Poet: William Wordsworth*. Baltimore: The Johns Hopkins Press, 1941.

HEATH, A. E. (editor), *Scientific Thought in the Twentieth Century*. New York: Frederick Ungar Publishing Co., 1951.

HEATH, T. L. (editor), *The Works of Archimedes and His Method*. Cambridge: Cambridge University Press, 1912.

HENDERSON, Lawrence J., *The Fitness of the Environment*. New York: Macmillan, 1913.

HERRICK, Judson, *The Thinking Machine*. Chicago: University of Chicago Press, 1929.

HEYDICK, B. A. (editor), *Americans All*. New York: Harcourt Brace, 1920.

HILL, Hibbert Winslow, *The New Public Health*. New York: Macmillan, 1916.

HITSCHMANN, Edward, M.D., *Great Men: Psychoanalytic Studies*. New York: International Universities Press, 1956.

HOVLAND, C. I., Lunsdaine, A. A., Sheffield, F. D., *Experiments on Mass Communication*. New Jersey: Princeton University Press, 1949.

HUIZINGA, Johan, *Homo Ludens: A Study of the Play Element in Culture*. Boston: Beacon Press, 1950.

HOGARTH, Basil, *The Techniques of Novel Writing*. London: John Lane The Bodely Head Ltd., 1934.

HURFF, George B., *Social Aspects of Enterprises in the Large Corporation*. Philadelphia: University of Pennsylvania Press, 1950.

HUXLEY, Julian, *Man in the Modern World*. New York: New American Library, 1927.

JAMES, Henry (editor), *William James—Letters*. Boston: Atlantic Monthly Press, 1920.

JAMES, William, *Pragmatism*. New York: Noonday Press, 1907.

JAMES, William, *Essays in Radical Empiricism and a Pluralistic Universe*. New York: Longmans, Green & Co., 1909.

JAMES, William, *Psychology*. New York: Harper & Brothers, 1961.

JEANS, Sir James, *Physics and Philosophy*. New York: Macmillan, 1945.

JOAD, C. E. M., *How Our Minds Work*. New York: Philosophical Library, 1947.

JONES, Ernest, *Sigmund Freud—Life and Work*. New York: Basic Books, Inc., 1953.

JUNG, C. G., *Modern Man in Search of a Soul*. New York: Harcourt, Brace, 1939.

JUNG, C. G., *Two Essays on Analytical Psychology*. New York: Pantheon Books, 1953.

JUNG, C. G., *Contributions to Analytical Psychology*. New York: Harcourt, Brace, 1928.

BIBLIOGRAPHY 168

KAEMPFFERT, Waldemar, *Explorations in Science*. New York: Viking Press, 1955.

KANT, Immanuel, *Critique of Judgement* (tr. J. C. Meridith). New York: Oxford University Press, 1928.

KARDINER, A., M.D. and Spiegel, H. M. D., *War Stress and Neurotic Illness*. New York: Paul B. Hoeber, Inc., 1947.

KARGER, Delmar W., *The New Product*. New York: The Industrial Press, 1960.

KARPINSKI, Louis and Winter, John, *Contributions to the History of Science*. Michigan: University of Michigan, 1930.

KASNER, Ed., and Newman, James, *Mathematics and the Imagination*. New York: Simon & Schuster, 1940.

KEATS, John, *The Letters of John Keats* (ed. M. Buxton Forman). London: Oxford University Press, 1935.

KESTEN, Herman, *Copernicus and His World*. New York: Roy Publishers, 1945.

KEYNES, Geoffrey, *The Apologie and Treatise of Ambroise Pare*. Chicago: University of Chicago Press, 1952.

KNEDLER, John Warren, Jr. (editor), *Masterworks of Science*. New York: Doubleday Books, 1949.

KOHLER, Dr. Wolfgang, *Gestalt Psychology*. London: G. Bell & Sons, 1930.

KOENIGSBERGER, Leo, *Hermann von Helmholtz* (tr. Frances A. Welby). Oxford: Clarendon Press, 1906.

KRAMER, Dale and Karr, Madeline, *Teen-Age Gangs*. New York: Henry Holt, 1953.

KRIS, Ernst, *Psychoanalytic Explorations in Art*. New York: International Universities Press, 1952.

KUBIE, Lawrence S., *Neurotic Distortion of the Creative Process*. Lawrence: University of Kansas Press, 1958.

LAIRD, Donald, *Increasing Personal Efficiency: The Psychology of Personal Progress*. New York: Harper & Brothers, 1936.

LANGER, Susanne K., *Feeling and Form: A Theory of Art*. New York: Charles Scribner's Sons, 1953.

LANGER, Susanne K., *Philosophy in a New Key*. Cambridge: Harvard University Press, 1942.

LAWTON, F., *Balzac*. London: Grant Richards, 1910.

LEEMING, Joseph, *Rayon: The First Man-Made Fiber*. Brooklyn, New York: Chemical Publishing Co., Inc., 1950.

LEMKIN, William, *Graphic Survey of Science*. New York: Oxford Book Co., 1954.

LEWIS, C. S., *The Problem of Pain*. New York: Macmillan, 1944.

LIBBY, Walter, *An Introduction to the History of Science*. Boston: Houghton Mifflin, 1917.

LIBBY, Walter, "The Scientific Imagination," *Scientific Monthly*, XV (1922).

LIFE (editors of), *America's Arts and Skills*. New York: E. P. Dutton, 1957.

LOCKE, John, *An Essay Concerning Human Understanding*. Dublin: Brett-Smith, 1816.

MACKENZIE, Catherine, *Alexander Graham Bell*. New York: Houghton Mifflin, 1928.

MACLAURIN, W. Rupert, *Technological Progress in Some American Industries*. Cambridge: M.I.T., Series 3, #13, Department of Economic and Social Science, 1954.

MACLAURIN, W. Rupert, *The Process of Technological Innovation*. Cambridge: M.I.T., Series 3, #8, Department of Economic & Social Science, 1950.

MACLAURIN, W. Rupert, *Patents and Technical Progress*. Cambridge: M.I.T., Series 3, #9, Publications in Social Science, 1950.

MACLAURIN, W. Rupert, *Investing in Science for the Future*. Cambridge: M.I.T., Series 3, #5, Publications in Social Science, 1946.

MACLAURIN, W. Rupert, *The Sequence from Invention to Innovation and Its Relation to Economic Growth*. Cambridge: M.I.T., Series 3, #12, Publications in Social Science, 1953.

McCOLLEY, Grant, *Literature and Science: An Anthology from English and American Literature, 1600–1900*. Chicago: Packard & Co., 1940.

MABEE, Carleton, *Samuel F. B. Morse—The American Leonardo*. New York: Alfred A. Knopf, 1943.

MACH, Ernst, *Scientific Lectures* (tr. T. J. McCormack). Chicago: The Open Court Publishing Co., 1895.

MACMURRAY, John, "Some Reflections on the Analysis of Language," *Philosophical Quarterly*, Vol. 1, 1951.

MALINOWSKI, Bronislaw, *Magic, Science and Religion and Other Essays*. New York: Doubleday, 1954.

MANVELL, Roger, *Experiment in the Film*. London: The Grey Walls Press, 1949.

MARCOSSON, Isaac F., *Anaconda*. New York: Dodd, Mead & Co., 1957.

MARITAIN, Jacques, *Creative Intuition in Art and Poetry*. New York: Noonday Press, 1953.

MARSHALL, Henry Rutgers, *The Beautiful*. London: Macmillan, 1924.

MASLOW, Paul, *Intuition versus Intellect*. New York: Life Science Press, 1957.

MATTHEWS, William (compiler), *Canadian Diaries and Autobiographies*. Berkeley & Los Angeles: University of California Press, 1950.

MATTHEWS, William (compiler), *British Diaries: An Annotated Bibliography of British Diaries Written Between 1442 and 1942*. Los Angeles: University of California Press, 1950.

MATTHEWS, William (compiler), *British Autobiographies: An Annotated Bibliography of British Autobiographies Published Before 1951*. Los Angeles: University of California Press, 1955.

MATTHEWS, William (compiler), *American Diaries: An Annotated Bibliography of American Diaries Written Prior to 1861*. Boston: J. S. Canner & Co., 1959.

MELLQUIST, Jerome, *The Emergence of An American Art*. New York: Charles Scribner's Sons, 1942.

MELVILLE, Lewis, *William Makepeace Thackeray*. London: Ernest Benn Ltd., 1927.

MILLER, Clyde R., *The Process of Persuasion*. New York: Crown Publishers, 1946.

MILLER, George A., *Language and Communication*. New York: McGraw-Hill, 1951.

MISCH, Georg, *A History of Autobiography in Antiquity*. Cambridge: Harvard University Press, 1951.

MOHOLY-NAGY, L., *Vision in Motion*. Chicago: Paul Theobald, 1937.

MORGAN, C. Lloyd, *Animal Life and Intelligence*. Boston: Ginn & Co., 1891.

MORGAN, C. Lloyd, *Habit and Instinct*. New York: Edward Arnold, 1896.

MORRISON, A. Cressy, *Man in a Chemical World*. New York: Charles Scribner's Sons, 1937.

MUNSTERBERG, Hugo, *The Americans*. New York: McClure Phillips & Co., 1904.

MYERS, Charles A., *Industrial Relations in Sweden*. Cambridge: M.I.T. Technology Press, 1951.

NERNEY, Mary Childs, *Thomas Alva Edison*. New York: Harrison Smith & Robert Haas, 1934.

NEURATH, Otto, Carnap, Rudolf, and Morris, Charles (editors), *International Encyclopedia of Unified Science*. Chicago: University of Chicago Press, 1955.

NEWCOMER, Alphonso Gerald and Andrews, Alice E., *Twelve Centuries of English Poetry and Prose*. New York: Scott, Foresman & Co., 1910.

NIETZSCHE, Friedrich, *Thus Spake Zarathustra*. New York: Modern Library, 1933.

NIJINSKY, Romola, *Nijinsky*. New York: The Universal Library, Grosset & Dunlap, 1934.

OAKLEY, Kenneth P., *Man the Tool-Maker*. Chicago: University of Chicago Press, 1957.

OATES, Whitney Jennings and Murphy, Charles, *Greek Literature in Translation*. New York: Longmans, Green & Co., 1944.

ORCUTT, William Dana, *Wallace Clement Sabine*. Norwood, Mass.: Plimpton Press, 1933.

ORTEGA y GASSET, José, *The Dehumanization of Art* (tr. Helene Weyl). Princeton: Princeton University Press, 1948.

OSGOOD, Edwin E., and Haskins, Howard D., *A Textbook of Laboratory Diagnosis*. Philadelphia: P. Blakiston's Sons & Co., 1931.

PACHTER, Henry M., *Paracelsus—Magic into Science*. New York: Henry Schuman, 1951.

PANOFSKY, Erwin, *Meaning in the Visual Arts*. New York: Doubleday, 1955.

PARE, Ambrose, *The Apologie & Treatise*. Chicago: Chicago University Press, 1952.

PARKER, DeWitt H., *The Principles of Aesthetics*. New York: Appleton Century-Crofts, 1920.

PASCAL, Blaise, *Pensees and the Provincial Letters*. New York: Pantheon Books, 1941.

PASSER, Harold C., *The Electrical Manufacturers, 1875–1900*. Cambridge: Harvard University Press, 1953.

PAULHAM, F., *The Laws of Feeling*. New York: Harcourt, Brace, 1930.

PEARSON, Hesketh, *Doctor Darwin*. London: J. M. Dent & Sons Ltd., 1930.

PIAGET, Jean, *The Language and Thought of the Child*. London: Routledge & Kegan Paul, 1958.

PIAGET, Jean, *The Child's Conception of Number*. London: Routledge & Kegan Paul, 1952.

PIERON, Henri, *Principles of Experimental Psychology*. New York: Harcourt, Brace, 1929.

PIGORS, Paul, *The Symbolic Significance of Management Decisions*. Cambridge: M.I.T. Department of Economics & Social Science, Ser. 2, #42, 1954.

PLANCK, Max, *A Scientific Autobiography and Other Papers*. London: Williams & Norgate, 1950.

PLEDGE, H. T., *Science Since 1500*. New York: Philosophical Library, 1947.

PLUTARCH, *Plutarch's Lives*. Chicago: Henry Regnery Company, 1948.

POINCARE, Henri, *The Foundations of Science* (tr. G. B. Halstead). New York: The Science Press, 1946.

POINCARE, Henri, *Science & Method* (tr. Francis Maitland), New York: Dover Publications, Inc., 1952.

POOR, Charles Lane, *Men Against the Rule: A Century of Progress in Yacht Design*. New York: The Derrydale Press, 1937.

PORTERFIELD, Austin L., *Creative Factors in Scientific Research*. Durham: Duke University Press, 1941.

PRINCE, Morton, *The Unconscious*. New York: Macmillan, 1916.

PUPIN, Michael, *From Immigrant to Inventor*. New York: Charles Scribner's Sons, 1923.

QUILLER-COUCH, Sir Arthur, *The Oxford Book of English Verse, 1250–1918*. Oxford: Clarendon Press, 1946.

QUINE, Williard Van Orman, *Mathematical Logic,* Cambridge: Harvard University Press, 1947.

RAYMOND, George Lansing, *The Genesis of Art Form*. New York: G. P. Putnam's Sons, 1893.

READ, Herbert, *Art and Industry*. New York: Horizon Press, 1954.

READ, Herbert, *Contemporary British Art*. London: Penguin Books, 1951.

REICHENBACH, Hans, *From Copernicus to Einstein*. New York: Philosophical Library, 1942.

REISER, A., *Albert Einstein*. London: Thornton Butterworth Ltd., 1931.

REYNOLDS, Sir Joshua, *Literary Works* (2 vols.). London: T. Cadell & Wm. Daves, 1797.

RICHARDS, I. A., *Speculative Instruments*. London: Routledge & Kegan Paul, 1955.

RIES, Estelle H., *Elias E. Ries, Inventor*. New York: Philosophical Library, 1951.

RIESMAN, David, *The Lonely Crowd*. New Haven: Yale University Press, 1950.

RHINE, J. B., *New Frontiers of the Mind*. New York: Farrar & Rinehart, 1937.

ROEDER, Kenneth D., *Insect Physiology*. New York: John Wiley & Sons, Inc., 1953.

ROSS, W. D. (editor), *The Student's Oxford Aristotle*. London: Oxford University Press, 1942.

RUSKIN, John, *Complete Works*. London: George Allen, 1903.

RUSSELL, Bertrand, *Mysticism and Logic*. London: George Allen, 1910.

RUSSELL, Bertrand, *Sceptical Essays*. New York: W. W. Norton, 1928.

RUSSELL, Bertrand, *The Impact of Science on Society*. New York: Simon & Schuster, 1953.

RUSSELL, Bertrand, *Philosophy*. New York: W. W. Norton & Co., 1927.

SANFORD, Hugh W., *Concerning Knowledge: Philosophic & Scientific*. New York: G. P. Putnam's, 1936.

SANTAYANA, George, *The Life of Reason: Reason in Art*. New York: Charles Scribner's Sons, 1903.

SANTAYANA, George, *The Sense of Beauty*. New York: Dover Publications, 1896.

SANTAYANA, George, *Three Philosophical Poets: Lucretius, Dante & Goethe*. Cambridge: Harvard University Press, 1910.

SAPIR, Edward, *Language*. New York: Harcourt, Brace, 1921.

SARTON, George, *A History of Science and the New Humanism*. Cambridge: Harvard University Press, 1952.

SARTON, George, *The Appreciation of Ancient and Mediaeval Science During the Renaissance*. Philadelphia: University of Pennsylvania Press, 1955.

SARTRE, Jean-Paul, *Existentialism and Human Emotions*. New York: The Wisdom Library, 1957.

SCHILLER, Friedrich von, *Letters and Essays*. Boston: Little, Brown, 1845.

SCHAFFNER, Dr. Bertram (editor), *Group Processes*. New Jersey: Madison Printing Co., 1954.

SCHILLINGER, Joseph, *The Mathematical Basis of the Arts*. New York: Philosophical Library, 1948.

SCHMITZ, L. D., *Correspondence Between Schiller and Goethe* (2 vols.) (tr. L. D. Schmitz). London: George Bell & Sons, 1879.

SCHROUDINGER, Erwin, *Science Theory and Man*. New York: Dover Publications, Inc., 1957.

SCHWARTZ, George and Bishop, Phillip, *Moments of Discovery*. New York: Basic Books, 1958.

SCOTT, Sir Walter, *Sir Walter Scott—Journal*. New York: Harper & Brothers, 1891.

SCOVILLE, Warren C., *Growth of the American Glass Industry to 1880*. Cambridge, Mass.: M.I.T., 1944.

SEDGWICK, William Ellery, *Herman Melville—The Tragedy of Mind*. Cambridge: Harvard University Press, 1945.

SEROFF, Victor, *Dmitri Shostakovich*. New York: Alfred A. Knopf, 1943.

SHEPARD, Herbert A., *Some Studies of Laboratory Management*. Cambridge: M.I.T. Department of Economic & Social Science, Ser. 2, #51, 1955.

SHEPARD, Herbert A., *The Value System of a University Research Group*. Cambridge: M.I.T. Department of Economic & Social Science, Ser. 2, #44, 1954.

SHEPARD, Herbert A., *Patterns of Organization for Applied Research & Development*. Cambridge: M.I.T. Department of Economic & Social Science, Ser. 2, #52, 1956.

SHEPARD, Herbert A., *Basic Research and the Social System of Pure Science*. Cambridge: M.I.T. Department of Economic and Social Science, Ser. 2, #53, 1956.

SHERRINGTON, Sir Charles S., *Man on His Nature*. New York: Doubleday Anchor Books, 1947.

SINGER, Dorothea Waley, *Giordano Bruno*. New York: Henry Schuman, 1950.

SMITH, Whately, *The Measurement of Emotion*. New York: Harcourt, Brace, 1922.

SNOW, C. P., *The Search*. New York: Charles Scribner's Sons, 1934.

SOUREK, Otakar, *Antonin Dvorak*. Printed in Czechoslovakia.

SOURIAU, Paul, *Théorie de l'invention*. Paris: Librairie Hachette et Cie, 1881.

SPEKE, John Hanning, *Journal of the Discovery of the Source of the Nile*. Edinburgh & London: William Blackwood & Sons, 1864.

SPENCER, Herbert, *The Principles of Sociology*. New York: D. Appleton & Co., 1898.

SPOCK, Benjamin, M.D., *The Pocket Book of Baby and Child Care*. New York: Pocket Books, 1946.

STEIN, Leo, *Appreciation: Painting, Poetry and Prose*. New York: Crown Publishers, 1947.

STOUFFER, Samuel A., et al., *The American Soldier: Adjustment During Army Life*. New Jersey: Princeton University Press, 1949.

SULLIVAN, J. W. N., *The Limitations of Science*. New York: Viking, 1934.

TAYLOR, Calvin W., *Research Conference on the Identification of Creative Scientific Talent*. Utah: University of Utah Press, 1955.

THOMSON, J. Arthur, *The System of Animate Nature*. New Haven: Yale University Press, 1920.

THOMSON, J. Arthur, *Darwinism and Human Life*. New York: Henry Holt, 1917.

THOMSON, J. Arthur, *Concerning Evolution*. New Haven: Yale University Press, 1925.

THOREAU, Henry David, *Thoreau: Philosopher of Freedom*. New York: Vanguard Press, 1930.

THOREAU, Henry David, *The Portable Thoreau* (ed. Carl Bode). New York: The Viking Press, 1947.

TILDEN, Sir William A., *Chemical Discovery and Invention in the Twentieth Century*. New York: E. P. Dutton, 1936.

TOYNBEE, Arnold, *The Industrial Revolution*. Boston: Beacon Press, 1956.

TUFTS COLLEGE Institute of Applied Experimental Psychology, *Handbook of Human Engineering Data*. Special Devices Centre, Office of Naval Research, Human Engineering Division, 1952.

TUNIS, Edwin, *Wheels: A Pictorial History*. New York: World, 1954.

TUNIS, Edwin, *Weapons: A Pictorial History*. New York: World, 1954.

TURGENEV, Ivan, *Literary Reminiscences and Autobiographical Fragments*. New York: Farrar, Straus & Co., 1958.

TUSKA, C. D., *Inventors and Inventions*. New York: McGraw-Hill, 1957.

TYNDALL, John, *Faraday as a Discoverer*. New York: D. Appleton & Co., 1890.

TYRRELL, G. N. M., *Homo Faber: A Study of Man's Mental Evolution*. London: Methuen & Co., Ltd., 1951.

ULICH, Robert, *The Human Career*. New York: Harper & Brothers, 1955.

VALLERY-RADOT, R., *The Life of Pasteur* (tr. R. L. Devonshire) (2 vols.). Westminster: Archibald Constable & Co., 1902.

VAN TESLAAR, J. S., *An Outline of Psychoanalysis*. New York: Modern Library, 1925.

WALLSA, Graham, *The Art of Thought*. New York: Harcourt, Brace, 1926.

WASHBURN, Margaret Floy, *The Animal Mind*. New York: Macmillan, 1917.

WEBER, Brom (editor), *The Letters of Hart Crane*. New York: Hermitage House, 1952.

WEINER, Norbert, *Cybernectics*. New York: John Wiley & Sons, Inc., 1948.

WEINER, Norbert, *The Human Use of Human Beings*. New York: Doubleday Anchor Books, 1950.

WHALLEY, George, *Poetic Process*. London: Routledge & Kegan Paul Ltd., 1953.

WHITEHEAD, Alfred North, *Adventures of Ideas*. New York: Macmillan, 1933.

WHITEHEAD, Alfred North, *The Aims of Education*. New York: Macmillan, 1929.

WHITEHEAD, Alfred North, *The Concept of Nature*. Cambridge: Cambridge University Press, 1920.

WHITEHEAD, Alfred North, *Science and the Modern World*. New York: Macmillan, 1925.

WHYTE, Lancelot Law, *The Growth of Ideas.* Zurich: Rhein-Verlag, 1955.

WHYTE, Lancelot Law, *The Next Development in Man.* New York: The New American Library, 1949.

WILLIAMS, Joseph J., *Psychic Phenomena of Jamaica.* New York: Dial Press, 1934.

WILLIAMS, William Carlos, *William Carlos Williams.* New York: Random House, 1951.

WILSON, G., *The Life of Henry Cavendish.* London: Cavendish Society, 1951.

WILSON, William, "Operational Creativity" Marketing and Transportation Paper #2, Michigan State University, East Lansing, Michigan, 1958.

WITTGENSTEIN, Ludwig, *Tractatus Logico-Philosophicus.* London: Routledge & Kegan Paul Ltd., 1960.

WOOTON, Barbara, *Freedom Under Planning.* Chapel Hill: University of North Carolina Press, 1945.

WORRINGER, Wilhelm, *Abstraction and Empathy: A Contribution to the Psychology of Style.* New York: International Universities Press, 1953.

WRIGHT, Frank Lloyd, *An Autobiography.* New York: Duell, Sloan & Pearce, 1943.

YOUMANS, Dr. William (editor), *Pioneers of Science in America.* New York: D. Appleton & Co., 1896.

ZIMMERN, H., *Schopenhauer: His Life and Philosophy.* London: George Allen & Unwin Ltd., 1932.

INDEX

DATE DUE

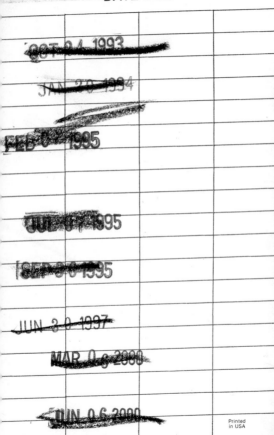

Printed
in USA